T0289146

# RISE OF THE
# UNDERDOGS

# RISE OF THE UNDERDOGS

## Football's New World Order

### BENCE BOCSÁK

First published by Pitch Publishing, 2024

Pitch Publishing
9 Donnington Park,
85 Birdham Road,
Chichester,
West Sussex,
PO20 7AJ
www.pitchpublishing.co.uk
info@pitchpublishing.co.uk

© 2024, Bence Bocsák

Every effort has been made to trace the copyright.
Any oversight will be rectified in future editions at the
earliest opportunity by the publisher.

All rights reserved. No part of this book may be reproduced,
sold or utilised in any form or transmitted in any form or by
any means, electronic or mechanical, including photocopying,
recording or by any information storage and retrieval system,
without prior permission in writing from the Publisher.

A CIP catalogue record is available for this book
from the British Library.

ISBN 978 1 80150 722 6

Typesetting and origination by Pitch Publishing

Printed and bound in UK by Short Run Press Ltd.

# Contents

Introduction . . . . . . . . . . . . . . . . . 7

1. Zambia . . . . . . . . . . . . . . . . . . 9
2. Canada . . . . . . . . . . . . . . . . . .25
3. From Côte d'Ivoire to Mali . . . . . . . . . .35
4. Croatia and Dinamo Zagreb . . . . . . .42
5. Japan . . . . . . . . . . . . . . . . . . .52
6. North Korea . . . . . . . . . . . . . .65
7. Jamaica . . . . . . . . . . . . . . . . .76
8. Norway . . . . . . . . . . . . . . . . .90
9. The Gambia . . . . . . . . . . . . . . .99
10. Georgia . . . . . . . . . . . . . . . 112
11. Ecuador . . . . . . . . . . . . . . . 121
12. Hungary . . . . . . . . . . . . . . . 130
13. Australia . . . . . . . . . . . . . . . 142
14. Morocco . . . . . . . . . . . . . . . 153
15. The New Age . . . . . . . . . . . . 161
16. The Republic of Ireland . . . . . . . 171
17. Egypt . . . . . . . . . . . . . . . . 180
18. Solomon Islands . . . . . . . . . . . 188
19. Luxembourg . . . . . . . . . . . . . 197
20. Saudi Arabia . . . . . . . . . . . . . 207
21. Uzbekistan . . . . . . . . . . . . . . 219
22. American Samoa . . . . . . . . . . . 230
23. Brentford . . . . . . . . . . . . . . . 249
24. Right to Dream . . . . . . . . . . . . 259

Acknowledgements . . . . . . . . . . . . 268

# Introduction

SITTING DOWN in front of the cameras after the conclusion of the 2022 World Cup group stage, FIFA president Gianni Infantino cut a proud figure. With a beaming smile and glowing eyes he announced boastfully, 'There are no more small teams and no more big teams. The level is very, very equal.'

Based on the performances in Qatar, few could argue with his statement. For the first time in World Cup history, countries from every continent had qualified for the knockout stage. In the group stage the likes of Saudi Arabia had conquered eventual champions Argentina, Japan had finished above Spain and Germany, South Korea were victorious over Cristiano Ronaldo's Portugal, and plucky Morocco had surprised everyone by beating a Belgian 'golden generation'.

As the tournament progressed, more upsets would be on the way and more history would be written. For the first time an African country made it to the semi-finals thanks to Morocco, who had beaten Spain and Portugal to get there. Meanwhile, Croatia had once again defied the odds and beat the likes of Brazil en route to collecting runners-up medals.

The events of that World Cup and previous continental tournaments, backed up by years of previous research, had affirmed my notion that things were truly changing in football, and that Infantino's words were not just mere gloating but backed up by actual facts.

Since 2019, I have been writing about underdogs and interviewing professionals in the game, focusing on this very subject as much as I could.

To raise awareness about the exciting changes and these innovators across the world, I founded a website called First Time Finish where I, alongside my co-founders Ninad Barbadikar and Tom Underhill, as well as talented contributors like George Rees Julian and George Hartley, covered football from Australia all the way to Zambia, focusing on how and why the game was developing in every region of the world.

In addition, I have been a frequent contributor to the *World Soccer* magazine and have had stories published in *The Guardian* and *Daily Mirror*, on GOAL.com, and was even cited by *The Times* to discuss these very subjects.

This book is the labour of all of that work and more that I have been doing for the last four years of my life.

The examples of the stories and people should not go unnoticed and can hold the key to the future of the game.

I have written about the players, clubs, academies and national associations who are building new frontiers and setting new limits. In doing so, I hope to quell some of the antipathy around the game and inspire hope.

I truly believe there is a new world order in football, but this is not a negative one. This is a new world order that is creating more parity and equality and contributing to the rise of underdogs.

# 1

# Zambia

*BA-DUM. BA-DUM. Bad-dum.* Isaac Chansa could feel his heartbeat ringing in his ears. *Ba-dum. Ba-dum.* He could hear the cheers of the crowd inside Gabon's Stade d'Angondjé stadium. *Ba-dum. Ba-dum.* Most of all he could hear his team-mates singing.

On 12 February 2012, as Chansa walked up to take a penalty in the final of the Africa Cup of Nations (AFCON), there was a lot at stake. But not for him, nor for his side, Zambia. Nobody had expected them to get to the final, let alone to hold out against a golden generation of Côte d'Ivoire stars led by the likes of Didier Drogba and Yaya Touré.

Somehow, some way, they had got there, and they were just a penalty shoot-out away from making history by securing Zambia's first AFCON victory.

'Before the match in the dressing room, the coach wrote: "Today is our day. On the 12th February we are going to make history. We are going to be remembered in the history books of Zambian football." That was his message to us,' Chansa remembered.

In the last seven AFCONs, before the 2012 tournament, Zambia had only gone further than the group stage on just one occasion. There were also just two European-based players in their squad for the 2012 AFCON.

Yet within the Zambian camp, there was a feeling of optimism even at the beginning of the tournament.

'We were looking forward to the tournament,' Chansa recalled. 'Looking back at our performances in the 2010 tournament, we had hopes that this time around we could go all the way to the final.'

Frenchman Hervé Renard had taken charge of the team for his second stint a year prior. At the time few outside of Zambia and African football were aware of his talent. After retiring from playing in 1998, he had been a bit of a journeyman, coaching from Cambridge United to Thep Xanh Nam Dinh FC in Vietnam. He eventually ended up at the helm of Zambia's national team initially in 2008. In his first spell in charge, Renard led Zambia to a quarter-final finish during the 2010 AFCON.

Going into the 2012 tournament, Renard had known his team's strengths very well. He was a driven and astute tactician and he had spent months preparing his team. Renard was determined to deliver the same level of success as two years prior, or even surpass that achievement.

'He made a huge difference. He changed our mentality,' Chansa said. 'He really pushed us in the training sessions. He is a coach who loves hard work. I remember he still woke up early in the morning to go running every day and he expected the same work rate from his players.'

During the 2010 AFCON, Renard's counterattacking football surprised many of Africa's giants. This time around he worked even harder to perfect it. Chansa and his team-mates were put through rigorous training sessions to hone every aspect of Renard's tactics. The Frenchman had also prepared his players with meticulous detail on each of their opponents.

Facing them in the group stage would be Senegal, Libya and Equatorial Guinea. It was a tough group that few even expected Zambia to even advance from.

'The mood was very fine. It was good. Just from the preparation for the tournament,' Chansa said. 'The coach had prepared us well. Especially for the first few games in the group stages, we knew those teams well.'

Zambia's preparation was clear for all to see in the opening game against Senegal. Renard's men took a two-goal lead in the first 20 minutes and held on to secure the victory.

Senegal tried everything to break down the resilient Zambian defence. This wasn't necessarily a golden Senegalese side, but it was still full of superstars. Players like Demba Ba and Papiss Cissé were the darlings of Tyneside at the time, having formed a formidable partnership for Newcastle United in the Premier League.

But Zambia's defence didn't give them a sniff at goal. Much of that was thanks to Renard having studied the two forwards.

'Before the game the coach Hervé Renard used to tell us about Papiss Cissé and Demba Ba because he used to work with them in France. We knew what to expect,' Chansa remembers.

'Our preparation was intense so we were ready and focused during the game. We followed the game plan and it went smooth.'

That victory over the far more favoured Senegal side gave Zambia a huge lift.

'After the game, we thought we had a chance to qualify from the group, that's what we were focusing on first. The win gave us a morale boost that we could do it,' said Chansa.

A subsequent draw against Libya and a victory against Equatorial Guinea followed, which was enough to see them finish top of the group.

Sudan proved easy opponents in the quarter-final, with Zambia running out 3-0 winners. The big challenge came against one of the favourites, Ghana, in the semi-final.

'The game against Ghana was something else,' Chansa recalled. 'That was our toughest game in the whole tournament.'

Ghana were full of Premier League and Champions League footballers. Senegal may have been full of superstars, but this Ghanaian team was superb, still widely regarded as one of the best sides Africa has ever assembled. They had reached the final of the competition in 2010, and had only grown in strength after a strong performance at the 2010 World Cup. Zambia knew what to expect. Renard had drilled the team's defensive discipline and for 90 minutes Zambia dropped deep, withstanding the barrage of attacks that came their way. Zambia's goalkeeper, Kennedy Mweene, was impenetrable between the sticks and thwarted several Asamoah Gyan efforts.

In the end, Zambia's patience and hard work paid off. Emmanuel Mayuka broke clear in the 78th minute and nestled the ball into the back of the net to give his team a remarkable victory.

'We were lucky and patient,' Chansa said. 'They [Ghana] were the best team, but because of our togetherness, and our belief in the coach's game plan, we ended up pulling through and scoring on the break.

'Once we beat Ghana, we told ourselves this was our time. Before even going to the final. We told ourselves God had given us this tournament.'

In the final, Renard's Zambia played the same tactic they had done throughout the tournament and frustrated Côte d'Ivoire's star-studded team, despite Drogba, Touré and the likes of Salomon Kalou and Gervinho putting in their best efforts.

Back home there were a lot of expectations for the latest Ivorian generation to finally deliver another AFCON victory after 20 barren years. With a team full of Premier League stars, those expectations weren't lofty either. That expectation weighed heavily on the shoulders of Côte d'Ivoire's big names, and it gave Zambia an advantage.

Back home in Zambia, even reaching the final was regarded as a huge success for the nation. There was no pressure on Chansa and his team-mates to do anything more, and that gave them the liberation to play freely.

'You could see the pressure on them,' Chansa recalled. 'In football it's easy if you are playing a big team, you'll be able to know the players and what they are like. We were underdogs and they didn't know anything about us. They had no idea what to expect. We were small but very hungry for success.

'At half-time the coach told us, "These guys are getting tired, and you are the fittest team at the tournament, so let's take them on. They will get even more tired if we can take them on to extra time, I'm sure we will beat them on penalties."'

Renard's words proved prophetic.

Fast-forward through another barren 45 minutes of football and then extra time, Chansa was walking those dreaded steps in the penalty shoot-out. *Ba-dum. Ba-dum.*

'I remember praying, calling to God to be on my side,' Chansa said.

*Ba-dum. Ba-dum.*

'But I felt no pressure. I was concentrating on the moment, singing in my head, looking at the goalkeeper and picking my spot. I put a bit of power and thankfully the keeper went in the wrong direction.'

If the game was tense, the shoot-out was something else. A total of seven penalties were taken by each team before Kolo Touré's effort was saved by Mweene. Rainford Kalaba failed to capitalise on that error, though, blasting his shot over the goal. At this point the pressure started to mount. Former Arsenal winger Gervinho stepped up next and missed his effort, gifting Zambia another chance. By then the shoot-out had lasted for over 17 minutes. For Zambia, 23-year-old Stoppila Sunzu was next. He stepped up to take the country's ninth kick and blasted the ball into the back of the net to summon an explosion of euphoria among the Zambians.

Chansa said, 'I could not believe it at first that we had done it. It was over. We were champions. That moment was crazy. I believed that this was our moment and then finally it came true. As we were running to celebrate together, I broke into tears of joy, celebrating talking to myself and God.'

In the annals of history, Zambia's 2012 AFCON triumph will go down as one of the greatest underdog stories in international football, up there with the successes of Greece and Denmark at the European Championship.

It would also inspire the next generation of Zambian youngsters already coming through the ranks.

\* \* \*

Few knew it back then, but Zambia's unlikely victory proved to be a catalyst for the country's football evolution. A decade later players like Patson Daka and Enock Mwepu would set a new frontier when breaking into the Premier League, and the national team would be filled with European-based stars in a stark contrast to just two members playing in Europe from Renard's 2012 squad.

Much of that change began a decade earlier back in 2002 when a fresh-faced college graduate, Lee Kawanu, returned to his hometown of Kafue. Kawanu had studied in South Africa but his heart brought him back home from his adolescent odyssey. Born in Russia to a Zambian father, he had grown up in Kafue since the age of two and he felt a special kinship with the town and the people.

'That's where I grew up as a kid and that's where my journey started from,' Kawanu said as he remembered his childhood.

Located 45km outside of Zambia's capital city, Lusaka, Kafue is a small industrial town home to just over 200,000 people – a small fraction of the country's almost 20 million total population. It is an industrial town, filled with factories that boomed during the 1960s and '70s.

'The town was mainly built around a fertiliser factory and a textile company that was built here,' Kawanu explained. 'It's a small factory town. Although, the factories are not as active as they used to be. Most people stay here and go to work in Lusaka now.'

When Kawanu returned home in 2002, his initial thoughts were not about football. He first ventured into the electronic business to try and diversify the town's infrastructure. He made money setting up his own company. But in the back of his mind, having grown up as a football-obsessed boy, the game was always on the back of his mind.

He said, 'My dad was a team manager for Nitrogen Stars, which is when my passion started [for football]. I remember my dad used to take me to games every weekend, sometimes we would travel with the players, so it was easy to just fall in love with the game at that kind of intimate level.'

When he arrived back to Kafue, one of the things that shocked him the most was that the beloved football scene Kawanu had remembered had completely changed.

'I quickly noticed that the activities that were there before, for example, Kafue having teams in the Super League or the First Division [the first and second tier of

Zambian football] were not there any more. The only team in the town were just playing locally in Kafue,' he recalled.

For Kawanu, still longing for the memories he made as a boy, he made it his mission to resurrect the football scene in the country. And an opportunity to do it fell serendipitously into his lap, 'One day two old men who played football in the past approached me and asked me to sponsor a team that they put together. Their thinking was to put all the best players together from the local area and make one strong team that we would then go and register with the Football Association of Zambia.'

This would form the foundations of Kawanu's and Kafue's legacy in Zambian football.

Kawanu admitted, 'Growing up you dream about owning your own football club, and then it happens. At first, I was not sure if I could do this, but I thought let me see if it's worth it.'

For Kawanu it was important to build the football club in the right way and to give back to the community, 'We named the team Kafue FC after the town just to get Kafue back on the Zambian football map.'

Kawanu also used the town's origins to form the club's mascot – a crocodile which also now adorns his club's crest.

'Kafue is by a big river called Kafue River, it's the widest river we have in Zambia, and of course there are some crocs there. I have always liked the nature of a crocodile; they have patience and the brute force when they need to pounce. So, it all tied in.'

It would prove to be a success story, as Kawanu continued, 'We started in the amateur leagues, and we went the whole season unbeaten and won promotion all the way to the second division.'

As Kawanu's success grew with Kafue FC, he gradually developed a feel for football and found he had a knack for building a successful environment from the ground up. When in 2008 the sponsors of nearby Lusaka Celtic pulled out, Kawanu was offered the chance to take over the club as well by the Zambian FA. At first Kawanu kept the two entities, Kafue FC and Lusaka Celtic, separate. But in the end, after just a year, he merged them together to make Kafue Celtic.

This is where the course of Zambian footballing history would be changed for ever. Now possessing two football licences, Kawanu built a first team and an academy, and he shifted his efforts on making Kafue Celtic a sustainable football club by investing in youth.

Kawanu said, 'Initially, when I started, I could not afford older players so over the years, I just got used to dealing with younger players.'

In 2009, the club sold its academy graduate, Chisamba Lungu, to Russian side Ural. Lungu was a part of the Zambian squad who would later win AFCON in 2012. He was Kawanu's first success story, and there would be many that would follow suit. Lungu's sale also provided an important learning curve.

'By then I started to learn that football could be a financially viable business other than something I was just passionate about,' Kawanu explained.

'I met a scout who used to work in Russia, and he told me players below 20 were all marketable in Europe, so that was the beginning for everything. At the time I rebranded, and I saw the need to start preparing players at a young age [for Europe].'

From beginning as a grassroots club just a few years prior, Kawanu eyed a totally different stratosphere and he got to work straight away, 'Our philosophy came together. We would have youngsters in the team. Have a youth system, develop a scouting system. After selling Chisamba, I realised I now had to look around the country, not just Kafue and

Lusaka, for players. I would watch school competitions with my coaches and see which players could fit into our team.'

But success wasn't always easy to come by; there were knock-backs and learning curves along the way.

Kawanu said, 'In the beginning I had special players, but they never ended up anywhere, because they had the wrong character. They would get too easily distracted, start drinking and just lose their way.

'So, after that, when I was scouting players, I tried to do more of an investigation into their background, what setup they are in, their families and stuff like that. I asked around to their coaches about how they behaved. Then when I was given the full picture, I would call him for trials, and they would stay with us maybe two weeks so that we could assess the character of the player first-hand and also whether they fit into our attacking style of play.'

Kawanu didn't just develop a philosophy in the boardroom, but also on the pitch. He quickly realised the best way to showcase his players' talents to scouts was by playing an attractive, offensive, possession-based style of football.

'We have always played a 4-3-3 from the beginning with as much speed and possession as possible. The way Liverpool or Red Bull [Salzburg] plays, that's what we try to copy,' he said.

Things gradually started to fall into place, and Kawanu began to receive attention, working his way up the ladder with Kafue Celtic, 'After a while I became an executive board member in the Zambian FA. They put me in charge of youth football and that opened my eyes up to even more opportunities. I had the chance to interact with people in all the provinces to help us with the national teams.'

Around the same time, Zambia had delivered that glorious AFCON victory. Football was on the rise in the country, and under Kawanu it was in good hands. But he still needed star players and top talent. He would soon find it.

\* \* \*

In 2010, Kawanu was watching Kafue Celtic with retired player Nathtali. The game was insignificant. Why Kawanu still remembered that meeting so profoundly many years later was not because of what happened on the pitch, but what Nathtali said to him in the stands. 'Lee, one day you are going to be happy with my son. And he's going to bring you big things.'

Kawanu didn't think much about the late Nathtali's words until four years later, when he went to watch Kafue Celtic's reserve team.

He recalled, 'I saw this really skinny, active boy on the pitch. He was shooting with his left and right, from outside the box and inside the box. So, I asked the reserves coach, who's this little kid? And he told me: this is Nathtali's son.'

The boy in question was Patson Daka.

Kawanu continued, 'Patson really caught my eye. So immediately I told the reserve coach to move him to the first team even though he was really small.'

Kawanu had found Daka just like he had found Kafue Celtic – at a time of need. Still a young teenager, Daka had lost his father a year prior, and had to cope with the difficult family tragedy. He found refuge in football and Kafue Celtic.

'He was really close with his dad. Nathtali was always really into football and he was a really nice guy and very talented too. He played football here in Zambia for Nitrogen Stars,' Kawanu explained.

Without a father figure, Kawanu became a crucial person in Daka's early career.

'Lee was always there to support me. He encouraged me and helped me make the right decisions,' Daka explained. 'He supported me and my family, making sure we had everything that we needed. He has been like a father to me, helping me to make big decisions when at some point I had to decide between football and school.'

On and off the pitch, Kawanu saw talent in Daka that he knew could take him far. The kind of talent Nathtali had promised all those years ago.

Kawanu said, 'You could just see an aura around Patson. It takes a lot for me to be convinced by a player. I've been around the scouting game for a long time. I scout all the players who come to my team because there is a certain character that I look for and Patson just had this thing about him.'

In return, Daka would help to take Kafue Celtic to the next level. But he did not do it alone. Around the same time, Kawanu also spotted another exciting young talent playing in Zambia's Copperbelt province by the name of Enock Mwepu.

Kawanu looked back, 'When I first saw him, he seemed a bit slow, but then I realised he moved the ball so quick. I think when you really look at him you realise, he is actually quite fast. He could eliminate defenders with ease thanks to his movement. His technique was excellent.'

Immediately, Kawanu brought Mwepu to Kafue Celtic as well. Born in the same year as Daka, the two of them would form the spine of the academy. With Kawanu's new role as a member of the Zambia FA, he also made them the spine of the national youth team.

In a bid to expose the players to new environments, Kawanu would arrange and embark on trips abroad with his talented Zambian cohort.

'We played Italy, Brazil and all these kinds of games. The boys were standing out in every game,' Kawanu recalled of the friendlies Daka and Mwepu played with the national team.

It was at these tournaments and then later at the under-17 AFCON where Kawanu and Kafue Celtic's fortunes took an even better turn.

Around the same time, former African Footballer of the Year Frédéric Kanouté had set up his own football management company, 12Management, with the sole mission and purpose to bring more talented African players to Europe.

An elite forward in his heyday, Kanouté took a liking to Daka and secured him trials with Red Bull Salzburg. The Austrian side took him on a six-month loan, where initially Daka struggled to adjust to his new environment.

'He found it very tough to adapt to the weather and of course the training is very intense at Red Bull. The constant pressing and high intensity. Nothing could have prepared him for it,' Kawanu recalled.

'But he is a strong kid, he never complained. Patson just said, "I'll make it." And he kept on pushing. He was always positive and believed that he would sign.'

By the time the 2017 under-20 AFCON came around, Daka was already at Salzburg, but Kawanu was convinced that Mwepu had the potential to join them as well. The tournament hosted on home soil in Zambia was the perfect occasion for Mwepu to showcase his talent and to follow suit.

Kawanu had advised his player to turn down lucrative offers from Qatar, South Africa and Spain in favour of holding out for Salzburg. As always with Kawanu, it would prove to be the right decision.

By 2017, Zambian football had been starving for success once again after the achievements of the senior national team five years prior. The core of Hervé Renard's great side were heading towards the twilight of their careers. Zambia needed new stars to inspire them and in Daka and Mwepu they found them.

Spurred on by the support of huge crowds, Zambia – led by Mwepu and Daka – marched all the way to the final, where they ran victorious over Senegal much to the delight of the adoring fans crammed into the Heroes National Stadium in Lusaka.

'They both had a crazy tournament,' Kawanu said.

Daka ended up as the Player of the Tournament and the top scorer. On the back of that success, in the same year he would be voted Young African Player of the Year.

But it wasn't just Daka; Mwepu also made his moment count.

'Everyone's eyes were always on Patson, but Enock was also sticking out every time,' Kawanu said. With the help of Kanouté, Mwepu was also recruited by Salzburg and the rest is history.

The two of them participated in multiple Champions League campaigns with the Austrian club, and both captained Zambia at senior international level, before making big-money transfers to the Premier League. In doing so they became only the third and fourth Zambians to play in the top tier of English football in the 21st century.

Unfortunately for Mwepu, that career was curtailed too soon. After being diagnosed with a heart condition he was forced to retire back in 2022, at the age of just 24 years old. A cruel blow to Zambian football, but even despite that setback, Kawanu has continued to work on helping more Dakas and Mwepus make it at the pinnacle of European football.

In the last few years, Kanouté had stepped into a consultancy role at Kafue Celtic, using his connections to help secure trials to the club's most promising players.

'Fred has opened us up to the rest of the world. He opened our minds to what it takes for a player to play in Europe. He has been very influential in the last six years that I have known him,' Kawanu said.

Meanwhile, Kawanu has built contacts in Europe to give his players the chance to play abroad and gain exposure to different styles of play at an early age. As a result, in the summer of 2023, Kafue Celtic toured Georgia and played in friendly games against Georgian teams.

The club also secured promotion to Zambia's top flight for the first time in 2021, another historic landmark to showcase how far Kawanu has come. Even after that achievement, Kawanu is determined not to slow down.

'The dream is what we are working on now,' Kawanu explained. 'I want to have satellite academies in each province. We are already trying to partner up with boarding schools in provinces.

'I'm hoping to start construction on a modern private school for privileged kids whose parents want them to learn football in an academy. But a section will also be for our elite players from all over the country who are most likely going to be underprivileged.'

Following his success, Kawanu has noticed he has had to face competition from new start-up academies, hoping to mimic his achievements. But he is not fazed. If anything, he has embraced the changes, and knows that it is all working towards the rise of Zambian football.

He said, 'My big dream is to have 20 academies like Kafue Celtic in Zambia. People say if you have competition, it's impossible to compete. But if we had 20 Kafue Celtics doing what we are doing, all we would do is open up even more opportunities and open up Zambia to the rest of the world.

'If we had that, everybody would know where Zambia is. With more academies running like us, we would have a bigger chance of qualifying for under-17 and under-20 World Cups, which will increase the value of our players and their visibility.'

The priority, though, will always remain to give back to the community as well. Kawanu will never forget his roots.

'Lee has played a big part in the community,' Daka said. 'He gave a lot of us young people a chance. He is someone who is very passionate about football and he means well for the team and the players as well. The relationships he builds with people and players is just something that is rare and one of the unique qualities he has.'

Daka and Mwepu were pioneers. Others have since followed them to top-level European clubs, like Fashion Sakala who signed for Rangers, Lameck Banda who moved to Lecce in Serie A, and Kings Kangwa who signed for Red Star Belgrade in Serbia.

With the country's European-based players continuing to grow year after year, Zambia continue to improve at senior level on the international stage. In the coming years the goal will be to emulate the success of the 2012 generation, and to go even further. Zambia have never qualified for a World Cup. Led by Patson Daka, and others, that elusive participation may now be not just merely a dream, but a tangible target. If Zambia ever get there, they will have Lee Kawanu to thank.

# 2

# Canada

CANADIAN SOCCER had never been famous for its successes, but in 2014 it had well and truly sunken to its lowest point. Without a goal in 958 minutes and without a win in two years, the country's national team had fallen to the depths of 122nd place in the FIFA world rankings.

During the previous two years Canada had been thumped 8-0 by Honduras and 4-0 by Denmark, as well as losing to Belarus and Mauritania, and they could not even clinch a victory against Moldova. Devoid of star players, devoid of inspiration, this was a catastrophic period in the history of the country. Back then nobody even dared to dream about the World Cup. It was all about avoiding defeat, and hoping for the best.

But in Edmonton, a young boy had different dreams, and in the ensuing years he would help completely transform Canada's footballing fortunes. That boy was Alphonso Davies – who has gone on to herald a new golden era in the history of the Canadian national team.

Alphonso Davies's story doesn't begin in Canada, though. If it wasn't for war breaking out in Liberia, Davies would have been born there, thousands of miles from Canada. Fate and tragedy intervened and his parents were forced to flee their homeland. Davies was born in a refugee camp in Ghana at the turn of the century – facing an uncertain future. The kind of uncertain future many millions still face today.

It was only five years later that Davies and his family would leave the camps and find a permanent place of refuge in Canada. By the time his parents settled in Edmonton, Davies was five years old.

Growing up, Davies was like most Canadian kids. A popular figure in school, he had aspirations to become an actor, and enjoyed sports. However, unlike most kids who grow up chasing pucks and skating on ice, he was only interested in the round ball.

From an early age, Davies was obsessed with football. His father played amateur level in Edmonton and young Alphonso would go and watch him play. He would dream on the sidelines about following in his father's footsteps.

Nick Huoseh has known Davies well. He has been his agent for many years, a close family friend and his former coach. He first saw Davies play when he was just nine years old and became his coach at a local club in Edmonton.

'Even at that age he was more mature than the other players. He was really passionate about the game. Some kids played just for fun, but he played because he wanted to be there,' Huoseh recalls.

The Canadian grassroots structure is not as easy to break into. Modelled on the US system, there are high costs that come with it, and pitches are not always accessible. In the years since Davies emerged on the scene, great strides have been made. But back then, Davies had to rely on the generosity of others to be allowed to play.

On top of that, he also had to contend with a tiring home routine. As immigrants, his parents had to hustle to survive and put food on the table for their kids. That meant sometimes both of them were away from home. As the oldest, Davies was tasked with taking care of his siblings, meaning there were times he simply could not afford to attend training sessions.

'His parents were both working shifts at different times. His mom would start late at night, 10pm or so and work night shifts. His father would start his work at four o'clock in the morning,' Huoseh said.

'Alphonso always relied on other players and their families. When I started coaching him I was picking him up and bringing him to training most of the time.

'I remember at ten or 11 years old he couldn't come to training or a game because he had to babysit his brother or sister, and you know most people that age are not even concerned about that.' Talal Al-Awad, Nick's assistant manager, recalled, 'So, he doesn't take anything for granted. For Alphonso, football was a sense of gratitude and appreciation. He respected the essence of the game, and he valued every moment he had on the pitch.'

As one footballing star was starting to grow in Edmonton, another was also starting to emerge on the other side of the country in Ottawa – Jonathan David.

Born six months before Davies, like his fellow Canadian star he also wasn't actually born in Canada. In fact, David's birthplace was the concrete jungle of New York. But he didn't see much of the Big Apple. David had been born to Haitian parents and his family moved back there when he was three months old. Like Davies, David spent his first few years growing up in a completely different environment than the place he would later call his home.

At six years old, the David family emigrated back to North America. This time their destination was Ottawa instead, much to the fortune of Canadian football.

Like Davies, David had developed a knack for the ball, rather than the puck, and he quickly became a star on the local pitches of Ottawa.

'He was as good as any ten-year-old I've seen. He had all the physical attributes,' Mike Lanos, Ottawa Gloucester Hornets' former technical director, recalled of seeing David for the first time after he had been tipped to bring him to his academy by a teacher from school. 'What struck me was how calm and chill he was. Nothing fazed him. We took him in right away.'

Like Davies, David also had to rely on the support of the community to get access to training and football in general.

'Football in Canada is expensive,' Lanos explained. 'Jonathan would not have been able to make it without the community's support. His family didn't have a lot and they were very grateful for what the community gave them.

'The teacher who spotted him sponsored him for a year, the next couple of years I sponsored him and then the club sponsored him for the remainder of his time.'

Without those contributions it is moot whether David would have been able to get as far as he did. But playing in Canada didn't just come with financial challenges: even the elements stood in the way of David and Davies.

For half of the year, Canadian winter makes it difficult for players to play on grass. Most games have to be played over artificial surfaces or indoors. This is one of the factors why football in the country is an expensive sport.

'Soccer is not a sport here that you can play year-round for free. There are no lit fields in Ottawa where you can just go to the park and play with your friends,' Jay Da Costa, the technical director of David's Ottawa Gloucester Hornets, explained.

'We only have a handful of domes here in Ottawa, and those dome times get used up, not just by soccer, but baseball and football and other organisations. It's hard to get that time and usually when you get it, you're definitely only training on one third of the field, sometimes even one sixth,' Da Costa added.

For Davies it was the same.

'He played indoor soccer quite a bit with us,' Marco Bossio, Davies's school coach at St Nicks, recalled. 'We had him training in our gymnasium playing futsal. Six months of the year he was training indoors because of the weather.'

But rather than being a hindrance, this would prove to be key for the duo's development. There are certain advantages that come with playing on smaller and smoother services.

'There was a flip side to that,' Bossio continues. 'There are moments now when he plays in the professional game when you watch him get pinned down in the corner and you think there is no way out but he manages to wriggle his way out the situation quite easily. I think that's a credit to playing indoors.'

Playing on smaller pitches with less space ahead of them, Davies and David learned to not only beat players with their speed but also to use technical skills to get around their opponents one vs one in tight areas.

Coupled with their determination, both would make a name for themselves in their local regions. Although the beginning of their footballing journey saw Davies and David follow a similar path, in their teenage years their route to stardom was starkly different.

From a young age, Davies had caught the attention of many North American scouts. One of the most crucial moments in his career would come at the Dallas Cup, an annual youth tournament hosted in the US, where the likes of Bukayo Saka, Wayne Rooney and Michael Owen had also competed in the past.

Davies's Edmonton Strikers had earned their call-up having emerged as a top side in Canada and the young teenager took his chance.

Talal Al-Award remembered, 'Alphonso performed really well in that tournament. He just dominated his opponents. It was the moment where we could measure and evaluate him against players at a very high level. We played against FC Dallas, Monterrey and Pumas in that tournament. They were some really big clubs. Alphonso performed amazing against FC Dallas. He scored twice against Monterrey. He really stood out.'

Immediately, Davies caught the attention of the scouts.

'Scouts from US colleges and MLS academies started to pay close attention to him in the Dallas Cup. There were scouts for the US national team who thought we were an American team and they started asking if he had a green card and they were a bit surprised and disappointed when they realised he was from Canada,' Al-Award continued.

Only 14 years old at the time, shortly after the tournament MLS club Vancouver Whitecaps started calling around to sign Davies up.

'I flew down with him to Vancouver,' Bossio recalled. 'We went down for a trial and as soon as they saw him play in the exhibition game the coaches didn't want him to leave and come back to Edmonton. He put on a show.'

Allowing Davies to move to the Whitecaps at such a young age was not an easy decision to make. Vancouver is roughly a two-hour flight or a 12-hour drive from Edmonton. He had to leave his family and everyone he knew behind.

But it was a decision that paid off. Just six months into his stay, he was handed a professional contract after catching the eye in the club's academy and earned a promotion into the second team.

'We didn't think six months coming into their academy he'd be given a contract. They had players there who were there for two years and at 14 years old he just came in and surpassed every kid that was there,' Nick Huoseh said.

At 15 years old, just four months shy of his 16th birthday, Davies hit an even bigger landmark when making his debut for the club's first team and becoming the second-youngest player in MLS history. Things developed quickly for Davies at the Whitecaps after that. By the time he was 17 years old, Davies was an MLS All-Star and was attracting the interest of clubs like Liverpool, Chelsea, Manchester United and Bayern Munich.

In the end, Davies, alongside Huoseh, opted to choose the Germans' proposal.

'They came with a plan,' Huoseh explained. 'They said we want to use him in the left-back position and on the wing, but more so we thought he would be up top on the wing.'

Moving from MLS to Bayern Munich, there was little expectation on Davies to make an instant impression. Historically, North Americans who had made the move from the MLS to Europe had struggled. But not Davies. He settled in instantly and became a pioneer, reaching a stratosphere very few North Americans have ever reached.

In a short period of time, Davies became Bayern Munich's first-choice left-back.

Huoseh said, 'When they saw him in training and saw how he could defend and how he was very good at it, I think that became his spot. We spoke about it and he told me they were going to play him left-back. I asked: do you care? And he said: no, as long as I play.'

Even in a more defensive position, Davies continued to have notable moments in the opposition's final third. His marauding run in the Champions League semi-final against Barcelona where he twisted superstars inside and out to set up an astonishing 8-2 victory back in 2020 was the highlight of the tournament that year.

Against all the odds, he propelled that Bayern side to victory in the competition, becoming the first Canadian male footballer to lift the Champions League, aged just 19 years old. Few would have envisaged him to do that when he first arrived on Canadian soil. But Davies is the epitome of the changing landscape of Canada and the growing popularity of the sport in the country.

In Ottawa, Jonathan David's journey has been equally pioneering, but at the same time it could not be any different from Davies's tale.

Unlike Davies, David did not give into the temptation of signing for an MLS club, as not just Davies but many Canadians do.

There were ample opportunities. Like with Davies, Vancouver Whitecaps were also keen to sign David. But unlike Davies, David, and particularly his mother, were not sold on the Canadian side's advances.

'They were speaking to me and to Jonathan's mother, and she was vehement that they were not in a rush. She wanted Jonathan to get his education,' Mike Lanos recalled.

So David stayed put in Canada, playing for the Gloucester Hornets in the provincial leagues of the country.

'By 16 he was starting to dominate the men's league and he finished as the top goalscorer,' Jay Da Costa remembered. 'Anything near the goal, he would just put in, you couldn't give him an extra yard around that 18-yard box. I remember, by that point, people were telling him, you need to get out of here. He was just far too good.'

It wasn't for a lack of interest that David ended up staying put. As well as Vancouver Whitecaps, teams like Montreal Impact and Toronto FC all made him offers and watched him closely. But David had set his sights on Europe, and he wasn't interested.

'He turned them all down,' Da Costa says. 'Everyone else in the Canadian national program was either in MLS academies or playing professional elsewhere. Jonathan was the only one who was just part of a community club.'

'He thought he was getting a good level of training here [Ottawa Gloucester Hornets],' Lanos added. 'He was part of the national programme too so he didn't feel like he needed it to leave.'

Instead, David held out until his 18th birthday, and went on a tour of trials around Europe from Red Bull Salzburg and VfB Stuttgart to KRC Gent. All three of them were interested in his services, but the latter gave him the best offer, and he joined the Belgians in January, a few days after his 18th birthday.

At Gent it didn't take him long to get going. Within two years, David had signed for Lille, helping the club lift the Ligue 1 title in his first season at just 21 years of age. Like Davies, in his own way David has paved the way for Canadians as well, and together they have created a new dawn for football in the country.

That new dawn was evident en route to the 2022 World Cup. Davies and David were the linchpins of a Canadian side that qualified for the finals with ease, securing only the second participation for the nation at the men's World Cup, and the first since 1986.

The tournament may not have reaped the rewards Canada hoped; they finished bottom of their group. But there were positives to take. Against Croatia, Davies became the first Canadian player to score at the men's World Cup, at just 22 years old. The goal was assisted by 23-year-old Tajon Buchanan, highlighting just how young the core of the team was at the tournament; David was only 22 years old.

Additionally, there was no shame in Canada losing to a 'golden' Belgian side, and opponents in Morocco and Croatia, who would both go on to reach the semi-finals.

Looking at the wider lens, the 2022 World Cup was a learning curve for Davies and co. ahead of the far more important showdown at the 2026 World Cup. That tournament will be jointly hosted on Canadian, US and Mexican soil. But regardless of what happens in 2026, Davies and David have already left a legacy that has inspired the next generation of young Canadian footballers.

'He [Davies] is a big inspiration and a huge motivator for aspiring soccer players,' Marco Bossio concluded. 'In the past they could have never imagined making it but now here's this young footballer playing in the Champions League and it's truly remarkable. There is a big poster of Alphonso in the gymnasium and it's an inspirational symbol for all of our kids; every time they walk in there, it's a constant reminder that they can reach their goals if they work hard and stick with it.'

Jay Da Costa said, 'I think it's going to grow [Canadian football]. Since Alphonso Davies won the Champions League title, I've had multiple players now, who are strikers, come up to me and say they want to play left-back. I think it's amazing, and a huge positive. These guys [Davies and David] are our current Wayne Gretzkys and Sidney Crosbys for soccer. And they're just young kids, which is amazing. I think the trajectory [of the national team] will hopefully be through the roof, and they will encourage a lot more players to pick up the sport.'

## 3

# From Côte d'Ivoire to Mali

IN THE early 1990s, Frenchman Jean-Marc Guillou had a dream – one that was different from the rest of his countrymen.

As a footballer, Guillou played from 1966 to 1984, spending his career in France and making over 500 appearances. He had even represented the French national team 19 times. But he always had ambitions beyond the pitch. From the mid-1970s, Guillou had worked as a player-manager, including at Nice and at Cannes. At the latter, he even appointed a fresh-faced Arsène Wenger as his assistant.

Working in France, though, was never his true calling. After four relatively brief managerial spells, Guillou had started to dream up a future away from his homeland.

In the 1970s, during the height of his playing career, Guillou had experienced a shift in French football, which was a reflection of society as a whole. Amid an economic crisis, the country opened its doors for mass immigration and allowed foreign-born individuals to permanently settle in France. As a result, some of the best players of Guillou's era were of African origin such as Salif Keïta, Jean-Pierre Adams, Laurent Pokou and François M'Pelé.

This would have a profound influence on Guillou. After leaving France and following a failed stint at Servette in Switzerland, Guillou had set out for Africa. Dissatisfied from his time in Europe, he saw Africa as football's new frontier. He had watched the likes of Keïta and M'Pelé become some of the best players in the French league, and he knew there was more talent in Africa waiting to be discovered.

Backed by money he had accrued from his playing days, Guillou had the financial means to support and establish an academy. So he set out for Abidjan, the capital of Côte d'Ivoire, and began work on building an academy from scratch.

It took several years to establish the connections and to build the facilities that would later make his JMG academy renowned all over the world. In the beginning he had been seen as a renegade. Not many would have backed his project to succeed. At the time, European clubs were not really looking to recruit players from Africa. But Guillou was determined. He believed in his project and he staunchly believed that there were thousands of players on the continent who were good enough to play in Europe – they just needed to be given the means to get there.

'We had prepared for about six years,' remembered Mamadou Wad, JMG's academy administrator, who worked with Guillou from the beginning.

In the six years Guillou spent raising the foundations of the JMG academy – the abbreviation being his initials – he established playing pitches, built a school in Abidjan, and then spent years travelling across the country to find the best burgeoning talent. During the trial process he had spread news of his academy through every available grapevine. Announcements about his trials were broadcast on television, the radio, and it was all the local kids talked about. Everybody wanted to impress Guillou and earn their place at JMG.

Among the first group of kids who attended those early trials was a young boy named Kolo Touré. Years later he would become part of an unforgettable 'invincible' Arsenal side in the Premier League, before going on to represent Manchester City and Liverpool. But back then he was just a kid who was obsessed with the game and often played with his father's military friends alongside his brothers.

'We organised the detection, we checked them for their weights and we watched them play. That's how we first saw Kolo, he was very good,' Wad recalled.

'Kolo wasn't easy on the eye, but he worked hard, that's what stood out. His mental quality and physical quality were very good. He had the mentality of a warrior.'

Signing Touré would prove to be a turning point in Guillou's career. The oldest of three brothers, Touré was definitely the first big prospect JMG produced, who didn't just cut the grade in Europe, but excelled and created a legacy few have in the modern era.

He also opened the floodgates and paved the way for other JMG graduates like Salomon Kalou, Gervinho and Emmanuel Eboué. But most importantly there was also Kolo's brother, who would go on to become one of the best midfielders to have played in the Premier League.

'One day Kolo said to Guillou,' Wad reflected, '"Coach, I think you have to take my little brother, because he is better than me and I think he will be taller than me."

'At first the coach said, "That's not possible." But Kolo insisted so Jean-Marc Guillou said, "OK, when you go home, bring your brother back to the academy."

'When Yaya came to the academy, Guillou turned towards him and said, "Your older brother said you are very good and you're better than him so I want to see you training for one week. If you are really good, I will take you."'

It didn't take long for Yaya to convince Guillou.

'In his first training when Yaya touched the ball, Guillou said, "Oh, this boy is good, he won't go back home, he will stay here with us,"' Wad remembered fondly.

The duo became the linchpins of JMG's golden generation. On and off the pitch the two brothers became role models for their fellow young prospects.

'For Yaya everything was easy,' Wad said. 'He was not very fast without the ball but when he had the ball he became a cheetah, it was impossible to get the ball away from him.

'Off the pitch Yaya was a big boy, he talked too much when he was not playing. He was always joking and laughing and spending his time with Ibrahim. Kolo was a bit more reserved, quiet and responsible.

'Yaya had more natural qualities than Kolo, but Kolo had the mentality of a warrior. Kolo wasn't easy on the eye, but he worked hard. His mental quality and physical quality were very good.'

The secrets behind Guillou's success relied on finding the best talent. Guillou is not just an accomplished coach: his ability to spot talent has been unparalleled in the years he spent in Africa.

'The coach [Guillou] says he makes his spirit empty before watching. He doesn't go to trials with any ideas. When he watches a player, he always tries to see what his "special quality" is. This is something specific that he cannot find with another player – that can be physical, mental or technical quality,' explained Wad of Guillou's methods for spotting potential talent.

When it comes to coaching, Guillou's principles are first and foremost focused on the mastering of technical skills.

'Guillou doesn't believe in just running and running. For him the football player has to play with the ball before anything else,' said Wad.

Unusually, in comparison to big European academies, Guillou has always worked with a small number of players. Every generation has around 12 and a maximum of 14 players at any given time.

Guillou's methods have come with some quirks as well. One of the most unusual aspects at JMG that the academy is renowned for is that the players play with their bare feet until their later teenage years, in order to be able to 'grasp' the ball better, according to Wad. They have always had to earn their boots by proving their technical ability first. When coming up with this concept, Guillou was inspired by the idea of how Brazilian players learned their technique by playing beach football barefoot during their formative years and wanted to create a similar environment at JMG as well.

'His philosophy is that first and foremost the ball must be a player's friend. It must become as natural to his players as using their left and right legs when they move,' Wad explained.

Guillou's methods worked. JMG's achievements in Côte d'Ivoire were pretty remarkable. The academy signed a partnership with ASEC Mimosas, and created a golden generation in the country which reached the World Cup for the first time in 2006 with 80 per cent of the players named in the squad having been developed at JMG. Impressively, the country then qualified for two more subsequent tournaments, in 2010 and 2014.

The group's greatest success, though, came in lifting the 2015 Africa Cup of Nations. After losing two finals and a semi-final in years prior, getting that victory was a huge landmark. But looking back, with the amount of world-class players the country boasted at the time, there are regrets at JMG.

'I feel that the federation of Ivory Coast could have managed the group better. This team should not have won just one Africa Cup of Nations, it could have been two or three,' Wad said as he looked back on the generation that he and Guillou helped to build.

Over the years, frustration with the federation in the country ultimately drove Guillou to pastures new. In 2007, a year after Côte d'Ivoire played in the World Cup for the first time, JMG moved camps from Abidjan to Bamako in Mali. It might have been a new location but the principles of Guillou remained the same.

Just like in Abidjan, in Bamako Guillou set up trials, an academy base and hired the best coaches. These were the secrets of Guillou's success.

But while the principles and methods remain the same, JMG has also made more attempts to work closer with the Malian federation, in the hopes that a potential golden generation in Mali will be better managed than the one produced in Côte d'Ivoire.

'We are trying to work closely with the federation,' Wad said. 'We don't want to make the same error as we did in Ivory Coast.'

More than a decade later, the fruits of Guillou's work have also been felt in Mali. Since founding the academy in Bamako, players like Yves Bissouma, Amadou Haidara and Cheick Doucouré have all made names for themselves in European football, and many other graduates are playing at top-level clubs as well.

At youth level, Mali have dominated not just African football, but on the global scene as well.

Between 2015 and 2019, Mali's youth teams were one of the most consistent teams at international level. In 2015, the country's under-17s won the first of two back-to-back Africa Cup of Nations titles, with the second victory coming up in 2017.

In 2015, the under-17 team also reached the World Cup Final where they lost to Nigeria. The under-20s came third at the World Cup in the same year, then won the AFCON in 2019.

In 2023, an exciting Mali team set the world alight by winning the bronze medal at the under-17 World Cup in Indonesia.

JMG graduates have played a key role in every generation's success at the respective tournaments, with at least four or five players involved in every squad. The stars making big moves to Europe have also often ended up being those nurtured at Guillou's academy.

What remains now is for Mali to continue that success at senior level. At the time of writing they have never won the Africa Cup of Nations, nor have they qualified for a World Cup. In this context the country's footballing history is very similar to that of Côte d'Ivoire when Guillou first arrived there. Now all that remains is for JMG's graduates from Bamako to emulate the success of their predecessors. Wad and everyone at JMG are not only confident in that conviction – Wad has made it clear – but that Mali has the potential to even surpass the previous generation made in Abidjan.

'I am convinced we will have the same success as we did in Ivory Coast,' Wad said. 'I think Mali could be one of the best teams in Africa for the next 15 years.'

# 4

# Croatia and Dinamo Zagreb

TO ROMEO Jozak's left, right and in front of him, Luka Modrić, Mario Mandžukić and Vedran Ćorluka were dressed in the baggy blue and white strips of Dinamo Zagreb.

This wasn't the Croatia dressing room during the 2018 World Cup. This was the early 2000s, before the cup finals and golden medals when the three men were just scrawny boys still learning their trade in Dinamo Zagreb's academy.

'Twenty years ago, all these guys were young and skinny,' former Dinamo Zagreb academy director Jozak recalled.

'When you go back and remember yourself in the locker room with all these guys it's unbelievable to think what they went on to achieve.'

Since the 2000s Dinamo Zagreb's diaspora has stretched across the globe. Jozak has seen the club's protégés including Modrić, Mandžukić and Ćorluka, lift multiple Champions League titles, World Cup medals and even a Ballon d'Or. Dinamo's work has earned them recognition from esteemed organisations like the CIES Football Observatory.

According to CIES statistics in 2021, Dinamo have produced the fifth-highest number of professional players (71) playing in Europe's top divisions. Only Real Madrid, Barcelona, Benfica and Ajax are ranked higher. For the training index, they are ranked fourth with a score of 77.9

with Sporting CP (91.8) , Ajax (102.3) and Real Madrid (81.4) ahead of them in the latest updated rankings.

Jozak, who worked in various positions at Dinamo Zagreb and the Croatian Federation for almost two decades, was instrumental in all those successes. Without him it is moot whether Dinamo would have the global renown and Croatia would have been as successful during the beginning of the 21st century.

It has not been an overnight success. Everything started back in the late 1990s and early 2000s when Romeo started working at Dinamo as an ambitious young coach.

At the time, Croatia was at an all-time high. In 1998, led by then Real Madrid forward Davor Šuker, the national team competed at the World Cup for the first time as an independent country. Having suffered a lot during the Yugoslav wars in the early 1990s, this was a nation starving for success and joy – which was what Šuker and his team-mates delivered. Croatia marched all the way to the semi-finals and won an unprecedented bronze medal after beating the Netherlands in the third-place match.

That victory was supposed to herald a new era for Croatia. However, for the ensuing decade they failed to really build on that success at senior international level. Croatia failed to get past the group stage at the next two World Cups, and in 2010 the country didn't even qualify for the tournament. For years it seemed like the success of Šuker's generation would never be repeated.

But behind the scenes Jozak had other ideas. Inspired by Šuker's success, Jozak realised the potential of Croatian football and he sought to create a strategy that would help the country reach the same heights once again.

His story starts just one year after the 1998 World Cup. In 1999, Jozak was a recently retired footballer who was working as the manager of Dinamo Zagreb's reserve team.

He was making tentative steps into the world of youth development.

It was during that time that he would discover one of the forebears of Croatia's next golden generation, and a future Ballon d'Or winner in Luka Modrić.

'Luka [Modrić] was good, he was very, very skinny,' Jozak recalled. 'He was agile and fast and he kept the ball securely like he does now. He played in the same position. To be honest, he wasn't standing out in the same way he does now but what he did have was stability and consistency. He was very reliable.'

Jozak had inherited a strong Dinamo reserve team which didn't just include Modrić but also Mandžukić and Ćorluka, who would all play key roles in Croatian football history for the next two decades.

'In the Croatian second league [where Dinamo Zagreb's reserve team played] it was tough, we played against a bunch of older guys who pressed us hard and the safest pass was always to Luka in the middle. He was never going to lose the ball or at least very rarely,' said Jozak.

At the time, though, Jozak didn't initially think they would reach the heights they then went on to climb. In the early stages even Modrić wasn't a spectacular talent who seemed destined to become one of the world's best.

Back then, Jozak remembered a Dinamo team littered with talented players, some who were on the same level as, if not better than, Modrić.

'In these early ages, he was OK, I mean he was more than OK,' he explained. 'But I tell you what back then we had 20 players in the second team who were all national players for the under-17s, under-18s and under-19 national teams. They were a bunch of really good kids who were the core part of the national teams. Some of his team-mates were just as good as him.'

Through the future Real Madrid midfielder, Jozak would learn a lot about football development. Having struggled to break into Dinamo Zagreb's first team, Modrić was sent out on loan to Zrinjski Mostar in Bosnia, where in a more physical environment he learned to adapt and grow as a player.

Gradually, Modrić used his experience in the tough environment of Bosnia's top tier to establish himself as a regular at Dinamo. Later he would sign for Tottenham Hotspur and then Real Madrid.

What Modrić's rise taught Jozak is that football development is unpredictable. Players must rise to the challenges thrown at them, but you never quite know who is going to make it until they are challenged and put to the test.

Like Modrić, Jozak also worked his way up the ranks at Dinamo Zagreb. After flitting around as Dinamo's assistant manager and a brief stint at NK Osijek in 2007, Jozak was appointed as the club's academy director in 2008 – incidentally the same year Modrić left for pastures new and signed for Tottenham in the Premier League.

'That was when things really began,' Jozak remembered.

By then Dinamo Zagreb already had a culture and strong academy ethos. Their first-team squad included the likes of Vedran Ćorluka, Mario Mandžukić and Dejan Lovren – all of whom would go on to achieve great success both at club and international level.

However, Jozak wanted to take Dinamo a step further. Having embedded himself into the club's culture, he had a strong vision of how to take Dinamo Zagreb to the next level. He wanted to create a new programme and a new way of doing things; a way to enhance Dinamo's model and to turn the club into one of the best academies in world football.

'In the first three years, maybe only two people stayed from the original staff who were there when I arrived. I said thank you and goodbye to 25 people in the academy,' he explained.

Jozak's concentrated vision necessitated radical changes. He wanted to bring in people with new ideas and fresh perspectives: coaches who were more aligned to his own modern football philosophy.

He continued, 'The criteria I was following with the new coaches was a particular personality. I was looking for people who had this genetic inborn passion, with a football logic and intelligence.'

Jozak spent extensive hours to put his vision together and assemble his backroom staff. He drove around Zagreb and across Croatia day and night to find the right personnel. He often listened to the locals, sought out talented coaches through word of mouth and went wherever all of those things led him.

'I followed their [potential coaches'] games in the lower leagues where they were playing, watching their behaviour in the game, listening to what others had to say about them without them even knowing,' Jozak said.

In the space of three years, as 25 staff members departed the academy, Jozak recruited roughly 32 new coaches. Importantly, he didn't just recruit coaches who qualified through coaching badges, but often went against the grain and brought in talented mavericks.

Jozak recalled, 'Some of them didn't have all the licences, but they had all the other things, like the personality, the drive and an intelligent understanding of the game. They had core human values which influenced my decisions.'

Jozak's decision has been affirmed in the years since, 'Those guys are now in the Croatian first division or later on became coaches in the Croatian national team setups.'

Changes were not just implemented in terms of staff: Jozak and his fellow coaches introduced an extensive training and development programme as well as an innovative talent identification system which is now being used by many other academies worldwide.

'I put down a curriculum where we concentrated about the skill and the technical aspects. One big component of that, however, was that the skilful players do not make it unless there was a mentality behind it,' he said.

'You can have all the quality in the world, but if you don't have the passion to put your head down on somebody's cleats it's going to be very hard to make it. So, we made sure we primarily selected players with a similar drive.'

The Dinamo Zagreb method was also ahead of its time in terms of incorporating scientific knowledge about muscle growth and cognitive muscle memory into the development programme. Jozak's subsequent material on the subject is still a core and essential piece of literature for budding coaches around the world.

'In terms of training philosophy, we created a periodisation and a curriculum to develop players' techniques at the right ages and not overload them, which at the time nobody else was doing,' Jozak said.

'In the ages of 11 or 12, we started with the basic operation of the individual technique transfer into the functional technique.'

An individual technique is what a player can do on the ball without the interference of tactics or opponents. Functional technique as defined by Jozak is when a player is using his skills to solve problems on the pitch. At Dinamo, the focus first and foremost was to develop individual techniques at a young age, before gradually moving to implement those techniques in more 'problem-solving scenarios' later on in a player's development.

'As the players grew older, we equalised functional technique with individual tactics. We taught players how to position themselves on the pitch towards the space and their team-mates in order to define their control of the ball,' Jozak reflected. This methodology was an integral part of the club's coaching system, 'The functional technique became a key component of our player development. At older age groups we used it to integrate it into team tactics to the offence and the defence. That was the general structure of our philosophy, with millions of details in there of course.'

To take one player as an example, Jozak explains the development of Borna Sosa. The Croatian international, who made a name for himself in the Bundesliga as one of the best crossers of the ball and even earned comparisons to David Beckham, is a unique talent. Sosa came through Dinamo Zagreb's academy, and was immediately spotted for his ability to cross the ball.

'Sosa had this talent with his left foot to feel the ball better,' Jozak explained. 'Together with all the other things that he had. But you know a lot of guys on the planet might be born with this ability [to cross the ball].

'We exposed him to different environments and situations all the time. Sosa had this talent with his left foot and the millions of repetitions that he did in different situations made him successful in every given situation that he is confronted by. That's why his crosses are so good.'

That's just one example of the meticulous work Dinamo Zagreb put into each and every individual in the academy programme, and how the use of periodisation techniques aided in the development of the club's young protégés.

With the right coaches in charge, an excellent player identification system and an advanced player development model, Dinamo were able to thrive under Jozak's tenure.

In 2013, the club's 1998 generation, which included Sosa and who were around nine or ten years of age when Jozak first took over, won the prestigious Nike Premier Cup, beating the best academy sides in world football including AC Milan, Arsenal and Boca Juniors at the hallowed Old Trafford stadium.

Since Jozak's tenure, Dinamo have also sold academy products to Juventus, Barcelona, RB Leipzig, Napoli, Inter, VfL Wolfsburg, Manchester City, Leicester City, AS Roma and Lyon just to name a few, netting the club massive profits in the process.

As a result, Dinamo's academy has become world renowned. In the last few years, not only have they produced a two-time World Cup medallist and Ballon d'Or winner in Modrić but also the most expensive defender in the world in Joško Gvardiol.

But Jozak's work hasn't just benefitted player sales: it has benefitted the success of the entire club, including the first team.

Always a historic club, Dinamo Zagreb were never a regular name in European football, until Jozak came along. Since his arrival, they have managed to regularly qualify for the Champions League and the Europa League, and they have even caused upsets, including knocking out Tottenham Hotspur from the Europa League back in the 2020/21 season with a starting 11 that had an average age of 25.6.

To get to these competitions, unlike other eastern European clubs who did it by acquiring foreign talent from abroad, Dinamo Zagreb have managed largely through integrating their own academy players and young Croatian talent into the setup.

'It's all about the coaches,' Jozak explained. 'All the other coaches and staff were just as crazy and had the same ambitions as me. It was together that we made the Dinamo Zagreb academy into what it is today.

'It doesn't matter which colour jersey you are going to wear, red, blue, green or whatever, you need a proper coach, with a proper drive, intelligence and the proper talent with strong values so he doesn't turn on the wrong path. Then you need the proper player selection and then the curriculum. That's the triangle which is very important for success.'

The club's prestigious academy has since attracted players not just from Croatia but all over the world.

Dani Olmo made waves when he switched from Barcelona's La Masia academy back in 2014 to Dinamo Zagreb in a move which has paid dividends to both the player and the club. In 2020, Wales under-21 international Robbie Burton moved from Arsenal to Dinamo at just 20 years of age.

'Fifteen years ago someone like Dani Olmo would never come to Dinamo Zagreb at the level the academy was when I got there. Now with all the references and our reputation around the world Dinamo can attract quality players,' said Jozak.

In 2013, Jozak left his role at Dinamo to take the helm at the Croatian Football Federation, where he worked on a nationwide curriculum which has helped the national team also improve its academy development.

Jozak's legacy endured in the senior national team as well. Fourteen players in Croatia's 2018 World Cup Final squad had either come through at Dinamo Zagreb or represented the Croatian giants during their careers. That number was a record at the tournament and will be difficult to beat in future competitions.

In the 2022 World Cup, it fell to 'only' 12 in Croatia's bronze medal-winning squad, but even that was a significant achievement for the club's academy. Another is the fact that from the 2010/11 season to the 2022/23 season there was at least one Croatian in one of the Champions League finalists' squads. This includes the likes of Modrić, Lovren, Mandžukić and Mateo Kovačić, who all came through Dinamo Zagreb's academy.

That decade-long run is a pretty remarkable feat. Few countries in the same period can match Croatia's record. For example, even England didn't have a representative in every single final during those years. The fact that this was achieved by a country of just less than four million people makes it all the more impressive.

In fact, relative to size and population, few countries have been as successful as Croatia in the world of football in the 21st century. The nation's success is a testament to Dinamo Zagreb and the innovative work founded by Jozak.

Whether the next Croatian generation can emulate the successes of the Modrić era and their predecessors is a chapter yet to be written. But there is certainly more optimism now that after two consecutive medals at the World Cup Croatia won't have to wait another 20 years for more success on the international stage as they once did following the 1998 World Cup.

# 5

# Japan

ON 24 October 1968, 100,000 people crammed themselves inside the Azteca Stadium. It was a cauldron. Fans adorned with green, white and red were everywhere. With sweat dripping from their foreheads, they waited anxiously to watch Mexico on home soil play against a very much unfancied Japan side for a bronze medal in the Olympics. As the game began, the crowd roared and echoed into the humid Mexico City night.

Japan's Kunishige Kamamoto heard the cacophony of drums booming in his ears. His team were expected to topple under the hostile environment, but he had no desire to succumb to defeat. Japan were there to make history.

Their run in the 1968 Olympics had been almost a decade in the making. It started with Dettmar Cramer, who took over as the technical director of Japan back in 1960. Tasked with improving football in the country, over the next few years the diminutive West German coach got right to it. Under his helm, the national team traversed Europe and held training camps in Germany. Initially, Japan faced humiliating defeats, losing by big margins. But over time, Cramer helped to instil a newfound understanding for football and hone the skills of his players.

By 1968 he was no longer in charge, and seven years later he would go on to win the European Cup with Bayern

Munich, but without him it is moot whether Japan would have ever made it as far as they did in Mexico. Cramer was very much the instigator of Japan's footballing success.

During the run to the Olympics bronze medal match, Japan had drawn with Brazil and Spain and beaten France. They had caused one upset after another, and they were confident of causing another even though they were up against the heavily supported home side in the Azteca.

When Kamamoto chested down a looping ball inside the Mexican penalty area and thumped it into the back of the net within the first 20 minutes, Japan made their intentions clear. Another 20 minutes later Kamamoto doubled the score from outside the box with a deft finish, sliding across the turf past the helpless Mexican goalkeeper.

Mexico failed to reply to Kamamoto's brace. By the end of the game, having grown despondent with the performances of their own team, the crowd had actually started to cheer for Japan. Over the 90 minutes, Kamamoto and his team-mates had won them over with their technical skill and desire on the pitch. They were the worthy bronze medalists and back home in Japan many celebrated the unlikely victory.

The nation's success at the finals was meant to herald a new dawn in Japanese football. But despite the initial enthusiasm, baseball continued to dominate in the ensuing decades. Football, meanwhile, failed to inspire the Japanese people.

There are many reasons behind why football took so long to take off in Japan. A lot of it has to do with the country's history in the 20th century and the popularity of baseball, which is still the number one sport in Japan.

Sebastian Moffett, in his book *Japanese Rules*, explained why this was the case, 'Japan approached the years following its World War Two defeat with a similar determination to pick itself up and overtake the west. Professional baseball teams were, of course, outside the realm of education, and instead resembled the ideal Japanese business, with disciplined, tireless workers happy to follow orders from above. As a play-by-play game, coaches played a large part in baseball, signalling from the bench how each move was to proceed.

'Far more than in the American game, the head coach's decisions were perceived in Japan as the crucial factor in winning. During live transmissions, TV cameras hovered on the dugout so commentators could size up the boss's expression and speculate on his next move. When the Tokyo Giants won the Nihon Series play-offs nine times in a row – from 1965 to 1973 – head coach Tetsuji Kawakami's method became widely known as "kanri-yakyu": "management baseball".

'Because his coaching and management techniques appeared to echo those of a successful corporate administrator, he understood the value of discipline in an organisation, made wise tactical decisions, and brought out the best in his underlings [the players].'

But that mentality started to change in the 1990s. Tom Byer, a former player in the United States, bore witness to it all. He had arrived in Japan as the first American to play in the Japanese league back in the 1985. The competition, called the JFL, was still semi-professional and his first impressions of the country very much echoed Moffett's observations.

'When I came to the country over 40 years ago,' Byer recalled, 'football was becoming more popular but there was no real footballing culture here. Even now it's not really there. What I mean by footballing culture is that when you go to Europe and you sit down in a taxi in Rome, the first thing you are going to talk about is football, about AS

Roma or Lazio. You weren't able to do that in Tokyo back in the 1980s.'

The Japanese national team had always been popular but the JFL had never taken off. The competition was run by teams made up of Japan's biggest corporations, like Hitachi, who Byer played for. All of the players belonged to the company, and only the top players were paid for playing. Others had formal and informal roles within the corporation alongside their careers in the game.

By the 1990s, though, Japan was changing. It had caught up with the west and became a dominant industry across the world, making technological and cultural advances that dictated trends.

For this new age in Japan, football seemed like a more apt sport. The game, after all, is about individualism: making independent decisions, showing off and becoming a maverick in the process.

As a result of these changing sentiments, the J.League was born in 1993 – the first professional football league in the country. During its toddler years it attracted players like Zico and Gary Lineker, and initially Japanese fans had taken to the game well, excited to watch foreign stars and local players.

The J.League also gave birth to the first Japanese football idol in Kazuyoshi Miura, who had returned from playing in Brazil for the likes of Santos to become the poster boy of the competition.

With the J.League driving the popularity of the sport in the country to an all-time high, Tom Byer had embarked on his own mission to herald a new Japanese era in the sport.

'I fell in love with Japan and I wanted to figure a way to stay here,' Byer recalled. 'So, I got into youth development.'

During his time in Japan and following his retirement from football, Byer became obsessed with player development. He became acquainted with the work of Dutchman Wiel Coerver and his 'Coerver method'. Born in 1924, Coerver is widely regarded as the 'Einstein of football', who introduced the first coherent concept of football development which advocated that 'skill' wasn't simply inherent in players but something that could be passed on through comprehensive training through a methodical structure. Under this technique, players progressed in a structured pyramidal manner, from learning the basics of ball mastery to a tactically driven group attack.

Struck by this new knowledge, Byer was eager to introduce Coerver's methods to Japan. Byer recognised there was a potential for the sport to grow in the country. He convinced Nestle to sponsor him and a few fellow coaches to travel around the country and teach Japanese kids about football.

'We were just working and doing kind of fun football events,' Byer recalled.

Over the next few years, through trial and error, Byer built up a philosophy and his own methods inspired by the work of Coerver. He had also become a popular figure among the local football scenes in Japan and in 1993 he founded his own developmental school.

'I was lucky to be in the right place at the right time,' Byer said. 'I started my schools in 1993. The J.League was born in around 1993 and the JFA soon put their hand in the air to become the 2002 World Cup hosts. Football mania was just nuts everywhere in Japan.'

Byer's schools became an instant success. Japan had taken to the game with a new wave of enthusiasm and excitement. The J.League became a sensation and stars like Kazuyoshi Miura – Kazu for short – became adored in the nation.

'I wanted to create this movement,' Byer said. 'I wanted to spread it out to as many people as possible. I physically did over 2,000 events for probably around half a million kids, parents and coaches. We had a very simple message: if you want to be a good football player, it starts with the technical component.'

Byer's own schools served as an important foundation. In the past, football had not been as accessible to Japanese children, particularly coaching at the level of Coerver's methods, which Byer had implemented.

That kind of high-level training was only readily accessible for baseball. But now Japanese children could attend Byer's schools and learn the basic foundations of the game at a much younger age.

Over time, Byer's business grew exponentially. In over a decade he had developed over 150 schools across the country, and had more than 200 employed coaches with up to 25,000 kids participating.

Players like Takumi Minamino and Wataru Endō, who both ended up playing for Liverpool, and former PSV Eindhoven winger Ritsu Dōan all benefitted from participating in Byer's schools, alongside many other future Japanese internationals.

In turn Byer became a popular figure in the country as the face of development in Japanese football. In 1998, he even earned a role on a popular children's daytime television show with a segment called 'Tom-san Soccer Techniques'.

'It was a show formed out of the Pokémon craze, so it wasn't a football show but a a pop culture show. I had my own segment and focused on a technical lesson in each one,' said Byer.

Byer's segment ran for an incredible 14 years, with him appearing every weekday morning in front of Japanese television screens to preach the basic principles of the game. However, popularity wasn't achieved just through his television show. Byer produced DVDs, along with having his own segment in popular newspapers, magazines, manga and comics. And he still put on big events, travelling across the country with his football school to spread the love of the game.

He said, 'It was a very simple message during these sessions. I was basically introducing this concept, one player – one ball and focused around ball mastering.'

On top of his advocacy for teaching Japanese kids the basics about the game, Byer also became an ambassador for Adidas in Japan and through his role he helped to build thousands of football pitches around the country to improve grassroots facilities.

By the time the 2002 World Cup, hosted in Japan and South Korea, came around, Byer was a key figure during brand events surrounding the finals.

The tournament was a seismic moment for football in Japan. The country had prepared for six years and there were high hopes in the build-up. Drawn in a group with Belgium, Russia and Tunisia, Japan surprised many with an opening-game draw against the Belgians. But then came the even more surprising victory over Russia and the subsequent three points over Tunisia, which saw the host nation top the group and qualify for the knockout round for the first time.

In the end Japan failed to capture the hearts of the neutrals as much as their fellow hosts South Korea, who made it all the way to the semi-finals, but a last-16 finish was still regarded as a successful tournament for a nation competing in just its second World Cup at the time.

The fact that Japan have managed to qualify for every subsequent tournament ever since, and make the last 16 a further two times in the last four World Cups between 2006 and 2022, is a testament to how significant of a turning point 2002 was for football in the country.

For many of Japan's modern-day stars who lit up the 2022 tournament in Qatar, it was also their first memories of the game. Take Kaoru Mitoma as an example. He was five years old at the time of the 2002 finals yet he still described vivid memories from the games in his autobiography *Vision*: 'An unforgettable present from my father was a "small soccer goal". In 2002, when I was five years old, I watched the Japan-Korea World Cup and instantly fell in love with soccer, so he built a small goal in the house for my brother and I.

'From the day a soccer ball arrived at our house, I was engrossed in playing soccer with my older brother, using the living room and the next room.

'I have been watching the World Cup ever since. The Japanese national team unfortunately lost to Turkey 1-0 in the last 16 [in 2002], but even though I wasn't on the pitch, I was able to rejoice with the Japanese national team players and feel some frustration as well. That's why when I was able to stand on that stage [in Qatar] where I always wanted to be I felt a deep emotion that cannot be expressed in words. I still vividly remember the powerful left-foot shot that Junichi Inamoto played against Belgium by dribbling the ball and forcibly evading the opposing defender.'

Japan's football development didn't just come about from the emergence of the J.League, the World Cup or Byer's influence. While all three have played a key role, the JFA has also been instrumental over the last two decades to establish important foundations and exposure for the national team's stars.

Since establishing the J.League, there are now three top tiers in Japanese football with relegation on the cards. That means there are 60 professional clubs in the country.

The national team became the first Asian representatives to be invited to the Copa América, in 1999. Japan have since been invited a further three times, for the 2011, 2015 and 2019 tournaments, only accepting the latter approach.

On top of that the development of the Kirin Cup, which was once a tournament played between top European clubs on Japanese soil back in the 1980s, to an international tournament over the last decade has been another key development.

Since 2018, the Kirin Cup has seen nations like Uruguay, Colombia, Brazil and Ecuador compete against Japan.

All those games will have provided key exposure to facing some of the world's top national sides and their top players to help Japan's players grow.

In the 2022 World Cup, Japan showed their modern might. To beat Germany and Spain, the World Cup winners from 2014 and 2010 respectively, was no small feat. To top the group was an even better achievement.

This was a Japan side that played with freedom and in the end was very unfortunate to bow out in the last 16 after a gruelling penalty shoot-out against Croatia. A quarter-final place still eludes Japan, but it is now a question of not if but when.

The make-up of Japan's squad in the 2022 World Cup was a very positive indicator of exactly that. Back in 2002, just four members were playing in European football at the time of the tournament. In 2022, there were 19 players from European clubs competing for Japan. Beginning from the 2002 finals, Japan's pool has grown remarkably in Europe.

'When I first came to Japan, over 35 years ago, there were always good technical players, but not the number of players right now,' Byer said.

'When we watched the national team play 35 years ago, we knew who the good players were in the starting 11, and when there was a substitute coming in we were like, "Oh, my God, they're not gonna put him in," because we knew the quality was going to go down. Now it's the opposite. We're like, well, why is you know who only on the bench? Why is he not in the starting 11. Now we have this endless supply of players. And again, the only way to make your best players better is by making the worst players better. That gap is so tiny here in Japan. Now when we're playing against Germany and we have an interchange of players, the level of play doesn't drop. It gets better. You got fresh legs off the bench and they terrorise the Germans technically.'

The impact of manga and anime culture cannot be underestimated either. Japan's previous generation had all grown up watching *Captain Tsubasa*, a show about a loyal, hard-working number ten whose goal was to win the World Cup for his country. Many Japanese players were inspired to play the game from the popular series, which also captivated famous international stars like Zinedine Zidane, Fernando Torres and Lionel Messi.

Today there is a new phenomenon on the manga scene in the form of *Blue Lock*, which conveys different ideals of football to the ones which Tsubasa set back in the 1980s. Created after Japan's failure at the 2018 World Cup, *Blue Lock* concentrates on Ego Jinpanchi, an eccentric coach, who vows to create a world-class forward for Japan.

In a bid to do so, he recruits some of the best high-school players in the country and locks them up inside a *Squid Game*-like facility where players compete against one another while being encouraged to develop their ego. The premise being that Japanese players lack 'ego', which prevents them from being the best in the world. Those who fail to overcome the challenges are booted from Blue Lock, and are subsequently exiled from ever being able to compete for the Japanese national team.

*Blue Lock* has become a sensation in Japan since its release and has been turned into an anime which was released just before the 2022 World Cup. Many now in the country see the new generation of stars as the 'Blue Lock generation' with parallels drawn from the anime and Japan's performance at the World Cup in Qatar.

Byer admits that the perception of Japanese players as team players comes with its disadvantages and advantages. Creating more individual players in the manner of *Blue Lock* can therefore help the game evolve and create more diversity in the national team.

'There's absolutely no doubt in my mind that as soon as people hear the words 'Japanese players', the first thing that comes to their mind is their technical ability,' Byer said.

'I mean, technically, they are very, very strong. They're also very, very disciplined. They're very organised, they are very coachable. They always put the team first. Japanese culture values team and organisation much more than individualism. In fact, we have a saying here in Japan that the nail that sticks up, you hammer it down, which is good and bad as well. There's some bad things about it as well.'

Previously, Japanese players were profiled as obedient and hardworking by foreign scouts. But the likes of Kaoru Mitoma, Takefusa Kubo and Takehiro Tomiyasu, as well as others, are certainly bucking that trend. While still hardworking, the aforementioned trio have a bit of egotism about them as well in their self-expression and free-flowing style.

It is no coincidence that Mitoma and Kubo both broke the Japanese goalscoring record in the Premier League and La Liga respectively for a single season during the 2022/23 campaign. There is a feeling that this generation can do better and fulfil the lofty ambition of a nation.

In his autobiography *Duel*, national team captain Wataru Endō echoed these sentiments of change, 'I think the appeal of Japanese players is that they can do what the coach tells them to do. However, if we only see the "good side" of this, we will ignore how this can be interpreted as just doing what we are told.

'As I have written, "player judgement" is the most important thing. Not all players think logically. It may be due to culture, upbringing and national character, but the individual abilities of top athletes are influenced by the ability to do things other than what you are told.'

Football, unlike other popular sports in Japan like baseball, requires a lot of individual thinking. Sometimes you have to make split-second decisions on the pitch, and you don't always have the answer or the crutch of holding on to tactical setups. Games are won by taking risks, and producing individual moments of brilliance.

As the likes of Kubo and Mitoma have proven, this is changing in Japanese football. According to Endō, the environment is changing inside the dressing room as well. Gone are the days when Arsène Wenger complained about his Nagoya Grampus players not being able to make decisions by themselves, and now there is an era of active discussions about tactics inside the dressing room.

'I think the current environment in which Japan's national team is able to exchange opinions and say, "Are there other options available?" is very positive. Coach [Hajime] Moriyasu always asks the opinions of many players, including myself ... Taking everyone's opinions into consideration, you can decide how to fight most effectively.'

Deference is still important in Japanese culture but the fact that the players are now capable of having open discussions has already reaped rewards. Communicating in the way Endō described is the key to creating the foundations for success, and Japan demonstrated that with their performances in Qatar.

There are also areas where Japanese football can still continue to grow and evolve. Endō sees one of the biggest areas of improvement in the physical aspect of the country's players.

'We need to be able to find the "optimal solution" for Japanese soccer,' he wrote.

'If you have "physical ability", you can become a great player. In fact, the top-of-the-top players who play for big clubs in the Bundesliga, Premier League and La Liga have a strong physical base, as well as technical skills, smartness and a high level of tactical intelligence. I think the Japanese soccer world needs to take more physical measures.'

The long-term ambition of the nation is to one day win the World Cup. Right now, that target seems elusive, but Endō believes that in the future it can become a possibility, only if the country focuses on smaller, more achievable ambitions first.

He continued, 'For example, it's still possible for the Japanese national team to win the World Cup, but I can't imagine it happening. This is because the "goal" for that purpose is not in sight yet.

'I'm sure that if the Japanese national team achieves the goal of making the quarter-final, then we will be able to reach that dream [of winning the World Cup] as well but things cannot be achieved by skipping one step.'

# 6

# North Korea

IN A conference room in Perugia, Liverpool's chief scout, Barry Hunter, was in the midst of a vehement presentation. As always, he waited carefully to deliver his final punchline. The trump card made everyone gleam and mouths drawn agape.

'You'll get to meet Steven Gerrard.'

Hunter waited in anticipation. But this time he did not receive the usual response. The recipient at the other end of the room merely sat with a blank expression on his face and stared back at him. He had no idea who Steven Gerrard was.

Mauro Costorella of Perugia's ISM Academy, recalled the moment Hunter failed to appeal to his protégé, 'The scout said, "Do you know Steven Gerrard?" But he just shook his head.

'The scout was very surprised. He said, "How is it possible you don't know Steven Gerrard?" The scout turned around and said it was the first time he showed a picture of Gerrard to someone and they did not instantly go "wow".'

Gerrard's name may be synonymous with those who love the game in most corners of the world. But the player Hunter was pitching to was Han Kwang-song, who had grown up in North Korea – one of the most repressive regimes in the world where access by foreign press and media is tightly restricted. Growing up, Han didn't have the access to watch Champions League or Premier League games in the same way the majority of the world does.

Fortunately, Hunter quickly got the gist, and spared Han his blushes.

'Everyone was laughing and Han was saying, "Sorry, sorry." But that is what Han is like, he only thinks about playing football,' Costorella added.

Unlike most stories in this book, Han's underdog tale is a complex one. It's fraught with political complexities and mysteries which shed light on one of the most isolated countries and people on the planet today. But first and foremost it's about a talented young footballer who, like many others in this book, had a dream, overcame a myriad of odds to write history and who came within a touching distance to accomplishing something even greater.

His story starts in the early 2010s. Back in 2012, the North Korean football federation sought to find a suitable European academy where the country's best prospects could develop and learn from their counterparts. Han's generation was one of the first – and, so far, only – generation to benefit from foreign influence. They first spent a few months training in Barcelona at Marcet Academy in 2013, before moving to Italy and Costorella's ISM Academy in Perugia.

'In the beginning the North Korean federation had an agreement with an academy in Spain, but the players only stayed there for one year, and they came to us instead,' Costorella said.

Italy was not an unusual destination for the North Korean team. The two nations' football history dates all the way back to 1966. At the World Cup hosted by England, they faced each other in Middlesbrough. Both teams needed a victory to advance from their group. North Korea, who were very much the underdogs, came out as the surprise winners, beating the Italians 1-0, which saw the country qualify to the quarter-finals. It was also the first time an Asian team had made it out of the group stage in the history of the World Cup – a feat that would not be repeated until almost 30 years later, by Saudi Arabia in 1994.

Ultimately, Eusébio's Portugal proved a test too mighty in the quarter-finals, with North Korea losing 5-3, but to this date that is the country's finest achievement on the world stage. That victory over Italy is still regarded as one of the most iconic underdog moments in World Cup history.

Italian politician Antonio Razzi was 18 years old when he saw North Korea beat his country in that World Cup. Later in life during the early 1990s and 2000s, Razzi would develop strong ties with the North Korean government, visiting the country several times. Upon one of those visits, he had the chance to meet North Korea's 1966 hero, Pak Doo-ik, who scored that famous winner against Italy. Razzi, with his strong ties, was influential in establishing the relationship between the ISM Academy and the North Korean government.

'It was a project made through Antonio Razzi and Alessandro Dominici, president of ISM's academy,' Mauro Costorella said. 'The North Korean federation were looking for a European academy to develop the players. In Italy we offered them what they were looking for, education visas and the opportunity to be scouted.'

The story really began to take shape in 2014, when the ISM Academy travelled to explore the football scene in North Korea and to find players who had the talent to succeed in Europe.

'Our delegation, represented by Alessandro Dominici, went to North Korea in 2014,' Costorella remembered. 'We had the intention to find the best talent.'

Given North Korea's isolation in comparison to the rest of the world, the ISM delegation was not really sure what to expect in terms of the quality of players they would find in the country. But they were blown away by what they saw.

'Technically they [the North Korean players] were perfect. We did not have much to teach the players in that regard, but tactically we taught them a lot,' said Costorella.

In the end, ISM brought back an entire team. Han Kwang-song was among them.

Costorella explained, 'We brought them here to a boarding school; they were given Italian lessons and accommodation. They went to school in the morning and then came to us to train in the afternoon.'

The North Korean youngsters were used to travelling and living abroad. They had already spent a considerable chunk of their development travelling to countries to compete in prestigious tournaments like the AFC Cup and trained in Spain at the Marcet Academy. Those experiences helped them to settle early into their new environment.

It wasn't long before ISM's team of North Koreans started to attract attention, first in Perugia, then across Italy and shortly all over Europe.

'We played games everywhere,' Costorella recalled. 'We played against Red Bull Salzburg and Genoa and we beat them. Everywhere we went people were impressed.'

The plucky North Korean team showed they were no pushovers, often getting the better of their opponents, even against professional adults twice their age.

'We went to play against a Serie C team, Maceratese; they were a side fighting for promotion, we drew 1-1 and they scored from a penalty. Our players were only 16 and 17 years old, it was really impressive,' said Costorella.

The North Koreans also drew with Inter Milan's Primavera side who were one of the best in the country at the time. 'They always put on a show,' Costorella said proudly.

Very quickly, word of the North Korean team spread in the local region. Among the people who were impressed by what they saw from Han and his team-mates was World Cup and Champions League winner Marco Materazzi.

'Materazzi lives in Perugia, so he liked to come to our games,' Costorella said.

Materazzi first saw the North Korean team playing a rondo in a training session. Instantly, he was mesmerised by what he saw.

Costorella revealed, 'He turned to me and said, "I have never ever seen such a fast rondo with my own eyes." You were not able to see the ball. You don't even see that kind of speed at a top club. The ball went from right to the left, and the player in the middle could not get near it.'

Even among such quality, Han stood out from the rest. Costorella, who took Han under his wing and even lived with the young star for two years, saw tremendous potential in the forward.

He recalled, 'Han was like a number nine with a fit of a number ten. He was very fast, one of the fastest players of his generation but at the same time he was a technical striker. The only thing he lacked was his finishing, because in North Korea the concentration was on the technical aspects like keeping possession and playing as a team.'

Coaches at the academy helped Han flourish and polish the weaknesses in his game. He was a hard worker, and both Costorella and Dominici were impressed by his professionalism and approach to training.

'He was always the first to arrive and the last to leave. He always put in the maximum, it did not matter if they were playing a friendly match or if it was Monday or Tuesday,' said Costorella.

Off the pitch, there were many curiosities and falsehoods spread about Han during his time in Italy. Coming from

North Korea, he was understandably heavily monitored by the state, but it didn't limit him entirely.

Costorella remembered a kid who was able to get a taste of the liberal and consumerist nature of a western country like Italy, 'He was an ordinary young man. He liked to hang out with his friends, to go shopping. But he never drank alcohol or went to party in clubs. He understood the type of lifestyle he needed to practise to become a professional.

'Even when he went to Cagliari and everyone was talking about him and he got a bit famous, he still remained humble. Every time we went to the cinema and people spotted him, he was always available to take pictures.

'If you brought them to do shopping or to eat Japanese food like sushi, Han and his friends were the happiest people in the world. Shopping and sushi were like prizes for them.'

In many ways, despite coming from a tightly controlled society, Han was just like any other teenager living in western Europe. But there was also a humble nature that came from his upbringing. There is no way of knowing the exact conditions of his life growing up in North Korea, but it clearly left its mark.

'He always remembered where he came from. He was from a normal family of workers. Everything he did and is doing now is for them. His dream is to be remembered in North Korea and Europe,' said Costorella.

Having spent many years in Italy, Han found a second home in the country, and very much embraced the lifestyle and culture.

'If you spoke to him, he'd tell you, "I'm North Korean, but I'm Italian as well." He lived here for four years; he can speak the language and cook Italian food,' Costorella added.

On the pitch, as Han grew more accustomed to Italy he continued to excel. Many clubs, including Liverpool, had followed the ISM Academy from around Europe. Manchester City were also close to signing Han, but in the end the political circumstances surrounding his homeland intervened.

Instead it was Serie A side Cagliari who took Han to professional football after impressing them during an initial trial, and it did not take long for him to settle into his new environment.

'When he went to Cagliari, he travelled there at 2pm. He ate a little bit and then he went to train with the Primavera team. The first day he scored a hat-trick in a friendly training match. So, they sent him to the first team,' Costorella recalled.

'In one of the first sessions with the first team, he scored in practice and he nutmegged [former Portuguese international defender] Bruno Alves.'

Han was still only 18 years of age. His ability to show such fearlessness caught the eye straight away.

'Han did not care who he was playing against, he just wanted to do well,' said Costorella.

Costorella revealed that one of Cagliari's first-team players, Daniel Desssena, was so impressed he told the club director he would buy Han himself with his own money if the director decided not to sign him.

'He scored a bicycle goal in one of his first games for the under-19s and from that moment he was with the first team,' Costorella added.

The rest is history. Han quickly settled at Cagliari. He constantly trained with the club's first team and showed he was more than capable of competing for a spot in the line-up, despite only being a teenager at the time. He played just three matches for the club's under-19 side before getting his debut in Serie A. In the process he became the first North Korean to play in Italy's top flight. A week later, in just his second appearance, Han scored his first goal, thus also becoming the first North Korean to score in Serie A.

In total, Han played three more times in Serie A for Cagliari until the end of the season. During the following campaign he was sent out on loan to AC Perugia to gain more experience. At Perugia he scored a hat-trick on his debut. He scored 11 goals and handed out five assists in 39 games for the Serie B side in total and it was enough to attract worldwide attention.

Some of the biggest clubs in the world once vied for his services. But most were deterred by the political ramifications behind a potential deal, which meant many pulled out of their pursuit. All except for Juventus, who decided to loan him in 2019, but the move was fraught from the beginning.

Costorella kept in constant contact with his former player. He remembered it was a frustrating time for Han: 'At Juventus, [manager Maurizio] Sarri really liked him. Han was always training with the first team and he got called up to the Serie A squad against Lecce, but then of course the political problems happened.'

Sadly, political problems have been a recurrent theme in Han's career ever since his breakthrough in Serie A. The UN has placed heavy sanctions on the North Korean regime right from the beginning of Han's journey in Italy, intended to suppress the country's nuclear missile project. However, it has had an impact on many North Korean citizens living abroad due to the precarious nature of their earnings.

'The North Korean regime sends thousands of workers abroad to work on construction sites around Russia and other places,' Martyn Williams, a North Korean expert from website 38 North and foreign affairs think tank the Stimson Center, explained.

'It's estimated the state takes about 80 per cent of their wages. They have no choice. With Han, it could be similar. If the state demands the money, he really has no choice.'

This is where things become murky. If the UN's estimates are correct, Han's wages paid by a club like Juventus could inadvertently help fund the North Korean nuclear programme. It is why the UN has urged its nations to deport all their North Korean immigrants.

One must understand why Han earning the equivalent of what a fellow young prospect would be receiving in wages at Juventus could be of a huge concern for the UN, and could indict football clubs. Violating UN laws would impose major financial penalties to any prospective club and would rule them as supporting the nuclear armament of a dangerous state.

It should come as no surprise that Han's transfer to Juventus on a permanent basis in January 2020 was short-lived. The UN immediately intervened and threatened sanctions. Six days later, Juventus were forced into selling Han to Qatar-based outfit Al-Duhail.

Despite impressive outings for Al-Duhail – Han made four goal contributions in seven starts and helped Al-Duhail lift the Qatar Super League – his career hit yet another dead end.

Han's transfer to Qatar was found to have violated UN sanctions as well and, as a result, he was unable to play for the club for several months before eventually being released. Since then, Han has tried to move to other clubs around Asia, but because of UN sanctions no one has dared to sign him.

'He is willing to go anywhere to play,' Costorella said.

But Han's situation is fraught. In a report by the UN, Han has insisted in official documents that he won't send any of his earnings back to the North Korean regime. Sadly, though, there can be no proof of his words. Even to

Costorella and ISM president Alessandro Dominici, the exact nature of Han's relationship with the North Korean government is a mystery.

'The relationship with the player we did not know, it was something personal with the federation. But he never had a problem with visas to travel back home and to travel here,' said Costorella.

In most likelihood Han is simply a victim; a mere pawn in a complex political game.

At the core, he is a super-talent who should have played in one of the top-five leagues in the world for years. Through no fault of his own, his career has sadly been stifled by a political situation which is unlikely to end any time soon.

On an individual basis it's hard not to sympathise. Sadly, it is the unfortunate harsh reality that Han and many of his countrymen have to live with.

During my conversation with him in 2021 Costorella hoped things would change soon and more North Koreans would get the opportunity to make a name for themselves in Europe. At the time, ISM's relationship with the North Korean Federation had waned but there were still hopes that it could be resurrected.

'We went to scout the players of the 2001 generation. There were some incredible players, but sadly their tutor died and the players did not come. Still, we are always in touch with the federation,' said Costorella.

For Han there is no happy ending. He disappeared for much of the pandemic only to resurface in 2023 during North Korea's 2026 World Cup qualifiers, playing in a 1-0 defeat against Syria and then scoring and registering an assist in a 6-1 victory over Myanmar.

Already he has lost years of his prime due to simply where he was born. There is little hope for him to return to

Europe with UN sanctions having tightened even further in subsequent years.

His only hope now is to make history with North Korea and help qualify the country to its first World Cup since 2010, and only the third tournament in the country's entire history. If he does that, North Korea will have Costorella and the ISM Academy to thank.

# 7

# Jamaica

CRAIG BUTLER felt the blunt edge of the pistol pointed at the back of his head. The men behind him were speaking in a language he did not understand. He was bruised and battered. They had blindfolded him and tied his wrists and feet. All he could feel was the scorching sand beneath his legs.

Trembling, he wondered, 'How did I get here?'

From an early age Butler only had one vision in mind – to revolutionise Jamaican football. With so much talent around him he was convinced there was more to Jamaica than one solitary appearance at the World Cup in more than nine decades.

This innocuous vision wasn't meant to end with him fighting for his life. This was just a game of football after all. Butler was just one man desperate to create a better life for his sons and to herald a new dawn in Jamaican football history.

So how did he end up in Mexico being kidnapped and within inches of losing his life?

It all began in Kingston, Jamaica. Butler's father had abandoned him and his mother when he was barely a few months old. Growing up, Butler was a lonely child and found his refuge in football.

His early memories as a kid were practising football with his grandfather in between coconut trees and heading the ball as hard as he could. Those early moments developed an infatuation for the game that has stayed with Butler for the rest of his life.

He recalled, 'Football was a big part of my life. It was a way of release for me. A way of getting out the loneliness that I had when I was a young man. I tried to use the football to heal my wounds. I played harder, trained harder. I didn't talk a lot.'

Butler wasn't unique in his way of using football as an escape. He recognised that many of the kids growing up in Jamaica sought refuge in the game, 'Our football culture, it's a release. It's a way of getting away from the guns, the violence and the poverty. You know, you forget that you're hungry when you're playing football. It's a great tool for us.'

Butler spent his teenage years and his early adulthood playing football in Jamaica and representing several of the country's community teams. He'd built friendships through the game with people like Peter Cargill – a Jamaican international who represented the nation at its first World Cup in 1998.

But while Butler was a successful player, he was also despondent with the Jamaican football scene. He saw talent around him lose their way, and saw that there was no way to make a stable income through football alone.

He did what many people do – leave. And went to study abroad on a scholarship in the US. But his heart always pulled him back to Jamaica. After his studies Butler returned to his homeland and became a general manager at Toshiba. Through his connections, just like his heart drew him back to Jamaica, football also kept pulling away at his heartstrings.

During his time at Toshiba, Butler organised and convinced his bosses to sponsor the Jamaican national team, and he was always looking for ways to help out his beloved sport as much as he could from afar.

As he grew older, Butler also started to understand the class divisions in Jamaica more profoundly. He saw poor neighbourhoods neglected and people from deprived backgrounds having more and more opportunities restricted. Even in football the biases were evident.

He said, 'Sometimes, you know, the kids wouldn't pass to the kid from the ghetto. And then if someone came from the ghetto and applied for a job at a big company even if they had all the qualifications in the world, they would be rejected if their address was from, for example, Arnett or Tivoli Gardens [two neighbourhoods that suffer from crime, poverty and drug trafficking], just because they are from a really poor community.'

Butler, having come from a difficult upbringing himself, felt the social divide acutely and he was desperate to change it. When his four-year-old son, Kyle, approached him and told him he wanted to become a professional footballer, Butler had an idea.

He knew football was a sport where you can create social parity and break down preconceived barriers within society. Butler didn't initially seek to revolutionise Jamaican football, but he was determined to create an academy where not just his son would thrive but everyone else, regardless of their background.

'I just started training them,' Butler recalled. 'Soon, more and more kids started to turn up.'

What began as a hobby quickly developed into a lifelong devotion for Butler. Initially, he kept his full-time job at Toshiba, but he started to consciously save up money and invest it into his academy. Eventually that became his full-time career and he established his now well-renowned Phoenix All Stars Academy.

In the beginning Butler adopted 23 kids from impoverished backgrounds and housed them in his own home. Taking on such an ambitious venture came with many struggles on the way.

'At first, I struggled just to find food. We were tossed out on the street by my estranged wife. She did not believe in my ambition,' Butler remembered.

'I fought hard each day to coach the boys, keep them focused and in school and find the money to grow the academy. I lost my vehicle to my then estranged wife and all our furniture so for a few months we were near homeless and slept on the floor of my sister's apartment.'

These were not ideal conditions to begin with but Butler never once wavered in his ambition. He continued to strive to provide for his sons and used his business acumen to build the academy from scratch, 'I managed to get some sponsorship from Clark, a huge phone company, and we were finally able to begin our journey.'

Among the first players adopted by Butler was Leon Bailey. Butler had found the then young boy, only six years old, begging on the side of the road. He stopped his car, took Bailey to a nearby Burger King and asked him what he wanted to be.

'A professional footballer' was Bailey's response. It was enough for Butler to take a liking to him and when he drove him back to his home in Cassava Place, he asked Bailey's mother if he could adopt her son and bring him to his academy. She agreed.

'Leon came from Cassava Place. It is on the side of a large gully and the houses were very poorly built,' Butler explained. 'It was a ghetto so to speak and poverty reigned supreme. It doesn't mean that bad only came from such a place because being poor doesn't make you a good or bad person – your choices do.'

Bailey was immediately among Butler's brightest students.

'At six years old most kids are not world-class players, so the first time he played he was OK. What was exciting for me then was his dexterity and his balance plus a constant focus and seriousness when it came on to learning what I had to teach him about football and life,' said Butler.

Butler had a knack for finding talent and nurturing it. Without prejudice he brought the best players to his Phoenix All Stars, and those in need of extra support he housed and fed.

He said, 'The primary focus of the academy has always been to use football as a vehicle to provide kids with a chance at a better life. In my academy players were and are being taught all the principles of business as well as the technique, skill and mental toughness needed to make it as a professional and/or to qualify for a scholarship at university.'

Butler's academy quickly developed a reputation within Jamaica. His side had won tournaments, beaten the best high-school teams and were attracting a lot of attention. He was starting to break the status quo set within the rigid Jamaican football structure.

He continued, 'We were not like one of the teams that have been there for years. But in a few years, we had the top four strikers in the country, the top four wingers and the top four defenders. They were all captains from our school team and they came from our academy and that was all built. It wasn't by recruitment. They actually grew up in Phoenix.'

As Butler puts it, his academy's success was both a blessing and a curse. Phoenix were the new kids on the block and they threatened to implode and radically change the Jamaican football structure that has existed for years.

'In Jamaica they created a hierarchy with clubs,' Butler said. 'So, the smallest clubs would sell quickly for little or nothing their best young players to the bigger clubs and if they didn't do it, the FA would come down hard on the little clubs, right?'

Naturally, through this structure Jamaica's bigger clubs tried to poach Butler's young stars. But most of them refused to leave his side. Having been nurtured by him for years, they were not going to leave their trusty mentor even for the allure of a more established team.

Butler said, 'The Jamaica football federation fought hard to break up our academy and to divide the players amongst the clubs that were members of JFF. Those who stayed loyal to Phoenix were ostracised and left out of the national youth teams. I was eventually banned in an effort to stop me from training and developing our players.'

This put Butler into a corner. He simply did not have any other choice left. Sitting up at night and staring up at the stars, he wondered what to do next. He didn't want to give up on the dream which he had worked so hard to build. Yet, inside Jamaica, he didn't have another choice, admitting that he had to leave the country. Once that realisation struck Butler, he began to prepare his adopted sons. Among them were Leon Bailey and three others. It was winter in Europe at the time and Butler knew the cold and harsh weather was nothing like they had been accustomed to at home. So, he made his sons stand in his local supermarket deep freezer to prepare them for the icy conditions which awaited them.

Their first destination was Austria. Butler and his four sons who had stayed loyal to him and were banned from playing in Jamaica – Leon, Kyle, Kevaughn and Travis – arrived in the middle of winter, flying in through the Austrian alps to land in Salzburg.

Surrounded by snow-peaked mountains, the family were shocked by the cold. Nothing could have prepared them for the way their misty breaths coiled visibly in the air, and how the icy wind stabbed at their faces. Not even the time they spent in the deep freezer was enough to imitate the harsh cold that faced them in Austria.

Butler and his boys couldn't turn back, though. Instead they put on layers upon layers of clothes to keep warm and trudged through the city centre from the airport to find a place of abode. The next day Butler was on the move again, hiking to Red Bull Salzburg's training centre with his sons.

They were met by bemused expressions when they arrived by the gate. But Butler begged to be let in. He had explained that his boys had come all the way from Jamaica, and in the end they were led to an office, where they were met by the academy director.

'You want a trial?' the Salzburg director said. Butler nodded, and the director shook his head. He was about to explain that this was not how things worked, but Butler was adamant. He kept pleading until eventually the director in front of him gave in.

One chance. That's all Butler's sons were given. They were led through the academy complex to be kitted and booted up and then straight on to the pitch. If this was a Hollywood movie, the trial may have been a scene of triumph for Butler and his sons at the end of all their travails. But this was only going to be the beginning of an uphill battle, and Butler quickly realised that.

'It was freezing,' Butler shuddered as he remembered the cold. 'During the trial, the boys froze on the field. They couldn't walk, let alone run. It was too much. I asked the director to give us more time to adapt, but he said no.'

The boys returned home defeated. Some may have sulked. They were away from home. They had travelled all the way across the other side of the world, only to be turned away. But Butler's boys were made of stronger stuff. They had not gone halfway around the world only to fall at the first hurdle.

'When we got home, the boys took off their T-shirts and ran three miles in the cold. We started the adaptation process the next day. We went to practise on fields and got used to the cold,' Butler remembered.

There would be more rejections for the youngsters as they tried to find their feet in Austria, but they never gave up. Even as Butler was struggling to make ends meet and had to resort to cleaning toilets and going without food to provide for his sons, their conviction never wavered.

'We went to almost every club in Austria,' Butler recalled. 'All the time the Europeans would say, "Jamaica? You mean *Cool Runnings?*" Or they would ask if we smoked weed. No one believed good footballers came out of Jamaica.

'It was so hard. The food was different. We didn't speak German and we had nowhere to live. We went from hostel to hostel. I had to take on jobs under the table to feed the boys.'

But when they had time to spare, the focus was always on their objective of making it in Austria. Every day Butler and his boys spent hours in the local parks training and practising while acclimatising to the weather as well. Butler was a staunch believer in hard work paying off, and he would be proven right.

During one of their practice sessions in the park, Butler encountered a director from second-tier club USK Anif. The director was impressed by his sons' dedication and the talent and invited them to a trial at his academy.

This time, the boys grabbed the opportunity first-hand and blew away the coaches during their trial sessions. USK Anif quickly snapped up all four of them and assigned them to their relevant age groups in the academy. Kyle and Leon even played an age group up.

Once they had settled at Anif, it wasn't long before the young players began to shine. Leon Bailey ended up finishing as the top scorer for the club in his first season in the Austrian under-15 league, and led his team to the final of the under-15 Austrian Cup, where a familiar foe awaited in Red Bull Salzburg.

'They won 4-2 in the final,' Butler remembered proudly. 'Leon scored two or maybe three, and Kyle got three assists.'

The game had been observed by scouts from around Europe, and it didn't take long before they started to approach Butler. He had offers from Salzburg among many other European top sides, who were determined to take his sons. But the best offer according to Butler was from KRC Genk.

During that period few clubs had been as prolific as the Belgians in developing talent. With a track record of producing elite players on the European stage, and an ethos which valued nurturing young talent and promoting them to the first team, Genk's offer was hard to refuse.

Butler said, 'I wanted the boys to progress. Genk was famous for Kevin De Bruyne, Christian Benteke and Thibaut Courtois. The technical training skills they had in the academy was what the boys needed to get to the next step.'

The move to Belgium saw Butler and his sons finally settle down in Europe. They had a consistent roof over their heads, and football in the club's academy was going well. All four boys were able to train with Genk's academy, while he landed a job as a sales executive with Austrian company Kickomat, which had developed a football delivery machine that could be used in training sessions.

To market the product, Butler was assigned to travel to Mexico and present it to a few professional clubs who had shown an interest. It was a difficult choice for Butler to leave his sons behind for the first time since arriving in Europe.

But with the promise of a stable income and commission, he decided to embark on a trip that would be life-changing, but not for the right reasons.

Shortly after arriving in Mexico, Butler found himself in the desert, kidnapped and stripped of most of his possessions.

He recalled, 'I was walking around like I used to walk around when I was at Toshiba with my nice suit and briefcase and they just came out of nowhere and scraped me off the street.

'They put a gun to the back of my head, beat me and took all my money. Then they put a blindfold on me and they took me out to the desert to kill me.'

Butler was convinced he was going to die. But in the end, through auspicious circumstances, with one of his kidnappers discovering the passports of Butler's sons in his briefcase, they decided to show mercy.

'They asked me, "What are these?" and I said, "Those are my children." The guy told me to go down on my knee. I refused. So, he hit me with the side of the rifle and I broke my knee. Another hit me on the side of the head. Then I heard them talking between themselves.

'They came back and told me to close my eyes and they put a gun to my head. They told me if I opened my eyes, they were going to shoot me.'

Butler kept his eyes shut for 40 minutes expecting his attackers to pull the trigger at any moment. When he finally opened them, he found himself alone in the desert.

'As far as I could see to the right, as far as I could see to the left, behind me and in front of me was desert,' he said.

It took around three days for locals to discover Butler. In that time, he came face to face with a rattle snake and survived without water. By the time he was taken into the hospital his kidney was close to shutting down.

'I kept telling myself I had to get back to the boys,' he recalled of how he kept himself going.

In Belgium, Leon and his brothers had no idea what had happened to Butler. They survived thanks to Butler's adoptive son Travis, who tended for the boys while Butler was away. But as the hours stretched into days without any contact, they too started to worry.

As soon as Butler was able to communicate from hospital, he contacted the boys and informed them of his safety. His recovery took months, and it was some time until he was able to return to Belgium. By then the landscape had changed around at KRC Genk. When Butler did get back to Belgium his residency was rejected and he fell out with the club due to personal matters, which meant he had to return to Jamaica with his sons.

By then Leon Bailey was 16 years old, and he had attracted the attention of numerous European clubs with his performances for Genk's academy. He was regarded as a top prospect in his generation in world football. Yet in Jamaica, Butler had to deal with the same limitations, which forced him to leave.

Despite Bailey's reputation and his performances in Europe, he was never selected for the Jamaican youth national teams during their return to the country. Butler remembered one frustrating occasion where he and Leon sat in the stands alongside a scout from Ajax watching the national youth team.

Butler said, 'When the Ajax scout was asked by reporters whether he had seen anyone interesting at the game, he said, "No." But there was someone sitting next to him in the stands.'

Instead, Butler and his sons spent two years training back at his Phoenix academy, preparing to return to Europe. By the time Leon had turned 18 years old, and was allowed to sign for clubs abroad as per FIFA rules, Butler packed their bags and flew to Slovakia to join Ajax's affiliate club, AS Trenčín, who had expressed an interest in his son and who had offered a coaching position for him as well.

They spent only a few months in Slovakia, months Butler doesn't look back on fondly. While the club provided them with everything they could, eastern Europe was a different world and they struggled to adjust to their new environment, encountering racism in everyday life.

In the end, Butler received an approach from KRC Genk. This time the Belgian club attempted to resolve the personal disagreement which had seen the family leave two years prior, and gave him an offer he could not refuse.

Back in a familiar environment, Bailey flourished. It took him just a few weeks to adapt to the academy and break into the first team. When he settled in, he didn't look back.

Over the next few years, Bailey established himself as one of the best players in Belgium, and first earned a lucrative transfer to Bayer Leverkusen before moving on to join Aston Villa in the Premier League.

Butler has guided his career throughout, becoming his intermediary, and believes there is still much more to come from his young protégé, 'Leon's greatest attribute is his determination and tenacity. He cannot be stopped. Once the coach believes in him he never lets you down. He was raised with the Phoenix spirit and mentality: never die, never give up, never stop and never back down.'

Bailey has become an icon in Jamaica. Few Jamaican internationals have made it to the upper echelons of European football in the same way as he has.

'Leon is the best Jamaican player who has worn the national team jersey,' Butler explained. 'He has accomplished the most and played consistently at the highest level. Having won best young player in Belgium [the Belgian Young

Professional Footballer of the Year award for 2015/16], then in Germany [VDV Newcomer of the Season for 2017/18] – it is no ordinary accomplishment.'

As Bailey's career has grown, so has Jamaican football. Since 2015, the country has made at least the semi-finals of the Gold Cup (CONCACAF's equivalent of the European Championship or Copa América) four times out of the last five tournaments. Previously, Jamaica had been able to do that just twice in the last 23 tournaments since 1963.

With three of Jamaica's biggest rivals in World Cup qualifying having automatically reached the 2026 finals in Mexico, Canada and the US, there is a good chance the country can end an almost three-decade wait to make it to the world stage once again. There will be three more slots from CONCACAF, and additionally two more places to make the inter-confederation play-offs – due to the expansion of the World Cup from 32 to 48 teams. Given Jamaica's rank in CONCACAF, their place at the tournament should be guaranteed on paper – although Bailey and co. will take nothing for granted.

By the time the finals come around, Butler may see more than just one Phoenix talent represent Jamaica. Since Bailey's career has taken off, Butler has returned to Jamaica to continue his work at Phoenix's academy and instil the principles he learned while in Europe.

His method is setting an example in Jamaica and Butler's success is there for all to see. In 2021, the same year Bailey signed for Aston Villa, Butler's academy went on a tour around England and beat academy teams from Crystal Palace and Aston Villa among others.

'Thanks to our work we have super-talents ready to break through into the professional landscape at Phoenix and who are hoping to follow Leon's path. Had we not fought, none of this would be possible,' Butler said.

One of those super-talents is Dujuan Richards, who became the youngest goalscorer in the history of the Gold Cup for Jamaica back in 2023, and who has a very good chance of following in Bailey's footsteps after earning a move to Chelsea from Butler's Phoenix academy.

'He is a game changer. He wins games by himself,' Butler said.

Having worked for many hours with Richards on the training ground, Butler also felt confident that he could live up to the same potential as Bailey, back when I spoke to him in 2023.

He said, 'I've seen him take on and dribble past an entire team and finish a goal. His lethal natural left foot is now matched by a more lethal developed right foot. We have basically created a Usain Bolt who can play football at the highest level.'

The goal will be to make the 2026 World Cup, but with talents like Bailey and Richards from Phoenix, the country may be able to do much more than that, especially since Butler continues to dedicate himself to the betterment of football in Jamaica, 'I am ready to keep going, to keep building and to keep hoping for a better footballing future for Jamaica.'

In the coming years, it is guaranteed more Jamaicans will follow the path Butler and Bailey paved through so many trials and tribulations. Thankfully for Butler, memories of his ordeal in Mexico are now just a distant memory. The next time he steps foot in the country, it may well be to watch his protégés take the field in Jamaican colours at the World Cup.

# 8

# Norway

BRUMUNDDAL IS about 140 miles north-east of Norway's capital, Oslo. It is a small and densely populated town on the eastern shore of the meandering Mjøsa, the country's largest lake. It isn't necessarily a footballing hotbed.

The town's football stadium is enclosed by towering hills wedged in between a rare expanse of flatland. There is a charm to the place, especially in the fall as the mountains mingle with the blue sky and the trees bunch together like a bouquet of flowers in a myriad of colours.

Norwegians go there to relax and wind back from the hustle and bustle of city life, to enjoy the scenic Mjøsa and the mountains which inhabit it.

John Vik, though, wasn't bothered about the scenery around him when he went to visit the town in 2015. He was there for one thing only – to find talented football players.

Vik had gone to watch an under-15 match between Norway and their fiercest rivals, Sweden. For a long time, this fixture had been an annual tradition for both sets of players. Traditionally, this is usually the first international game of their careers. It's a rite of passage; a game when the young boys grow into men.

Vik had watched a lot of these affairs. He had developed a good eye for talent. He'd scouted players for Molde FK, one of the country's biggest teams, and worked for Ole Gunnar Solskjær at Cardiff City. But even he was mesmerised by what he saw unfold on the pitch during that fateful day in 2015. He saw something special in the form of a scrawny boy from Bryn called Erling Haaland.

'Mentally he looked on a different planet,' Vik recalled to me in 2020.

'It's the first game you play on the home ground, you have the national team shirt on, your parents and family are in the stands. There's a lot of pressure. And some players hide a bit. They just play simple football, nothing extra, but he did not hide at all. He looked like he was born for that kind of stage.'

It's difficult to pinpoint what impressed Vik the most about Haaland, though there is one moment that has lived vividly in his memory even many years later.

In the second half when Norway prepared to restart the match, Haaland stood in the centre circle and caught the Swedish keeper standing off his line. He didn't hesitate and unleashed a powerful shot on goal. *Thwack. Whoosh. Thump.* It flew over the ambling goalkeeper and nestled into the back of the net leaving the crowd in Brumunddal stunned, and the young forward feeling very smug.

Vik recalled, 'I saw him talking to his team-mate and I thought, no, he's not going to try that, but Erling put the ball straight into the goal. It wasn't the technical part that was impressive, but rather the balls that he even dared to try something like that.'

From that moment, Vik knew he had found someone special, and like any diligent scout he kept a close eye on Haaland's development in the following months, 'I watched him as much as I could, especially for the national team. He has a head that is different than other boys, he is so unafraid and that's why I became so interested in him.'

Vik was determined to take Haaland to Molde. He saw the potential in the young boy, which not many others saw at the time.

He said, 'I didn't want to sell him but I spoke to a lot of top English clubs during the national team games and I told them to keep an eye on him and they said, "No, he's just a target man, nothing special." So, we [Molde] didn't have competition [to sign Haaland] from abroad.'

About a year and a half of relentless scouting later, Molde and Haaland would finally join forces in what Vik described as the 'perfect' union, 'In the end we invited him to training, showed him the club, he met the gaffer [Solskjær] and we showed him that we could be a decent place for him to go. We signed him peacefully; when the push came to shove no one else showed up.'

Looking back at all Haaland has achieved in the game, it's remarkable that at the time Molde were able to lure him with such ease. In a way it was almost fate. At the time few would have been as attentive to Haaland as Molde. At the club, Haaland underwent a metamorphosis and huge physical transformation. He grew several inches in height and bulked up in muscle as well.

The club managed him carefully as he underwent his growth spurt, providing him with nutrition and regular intense sessions in the gym. At the same time, Haaland was also prevented from training with the rest of the team, as a precaution to make sure his body developed in the right way.

Vik recalled, 'He grew 11, 12 centimetres in a year, and he was very lucky because most boys just grow and become really skinny, but he grew with weight as well. So, we kept him away from training and he was really impatient, because we wouldn't play him, he didn't get games, he just had to train alternatively for a long time. The medical department felt that the best thing for him was to take it easy for the next maybe six months and slowly, slowly put him back into football.'

It wasn't just a physical transformation, though. Moving all the way across Norway to the other side of the country was a huge learning curve as well. It taught Haaland to grow up faster than most kids his age.

Vik said, 'He was also very mature for his age. I remember speaking to him on the training ground and I asked about his living situation and he told me he lived alone and I asked him about his laundry and food and he just looked at me funny. "I do it myself," he said. "You think I'm an idiot?" I know a lot of 16-year-olds, most of them are not doing that stuff.'

Once overcoming that frustrating period, there was no stopping Haaland. He became a machine at Molde and won his team-mates over, on and off the pitch.

'He was a kid who was longing to express himself, people loved him at the club, very strong socially, he made a lot of friends at the club,' Vik said.

The rest is history. Haaland became a superhuman, breaking one record after another, from scoring nine goals in a single under-20 World Cup game against Honduras – a FIFA record – to scoring a first-half hat-trick on his debut in the Champions League and breaking the Premier League goalscoring record in a single season.

Haaland's rise has also given hope to Norwegian football. When he emerged, Norway had not qualified for a major tournament for more than 20 years. On the scale of probability, the chance of the country producing one of the best players on the planet who would go on to finish in second place behind Lionel Messi in the 2023 Ballon d'Or race was astronomically small.

But Haaland's emergence in Norway is not an anomaly. It's a pattern of the country's football evolution. The

Norwegian generation which has emerged in the 2020s has been an exciting group. It includes Arsenal captain Martin Ødegaard, who at 14 years old was already playing first-team football and by 16 had signed for Real Madrid.

'We've been writing about Ødegaard for so many years, and then Erling came,' Vik remembered. 'I think the two of them will be our biggest stars. This is a good period for Norway without a doubt.'

On top of Norway's two stars, there's also Leo Østigård, who in 2023 played a role in helping Napoli win Serie A for the first time in 33 years. In the same year, Julian Ryerson was part of a Borussia Dortmund team that came the closest to pushing Bayern Munich for the Bundesliga title. The pair were aged only 23 and 25 respectively.

That same season, Antonio Nusa became the second-youngest player to score in the Champions League at just 17 years and five months, and Andreas Schjelderup signed for Benfica with the club immediately setting a €100m release clause in his contract.

This level of talent isn't necessarily a new phenomenon. Norway has always had a handful of top talents at the upper echelons of the game. In the 1990s and early 2000s there was a booming golden generation which beat Brazil and was even ranked in second place in the FIFA world list at one point in 1993. During that period Norway regularly competed at major tournaments, and qualified for the World Cups of 1994 and 1998.

But then the turn of the century heralded a decade of slump. As the golden generation faded into oblivion, Norway's success dried up. As of the summer of 2024, they had not qualified for an international tournament since Euro 2000.

But while on-pitch success has been difficult to achieve, behind the scenes the authorities have been busy working to establish a new golden generation. Using the foundations that the old guard established and the path they have paved, the country has invested into grassroots football and created a development programme that has enabled the environment for players like Haaland and Ødegaard to emerge.

Since the 1990s, Norway has grown in prosperity. It is one of the richest countries in the world – in terms of GDP per capita, the country was ranked in fifth place by an IMF report in 2023. A lot of Norway's economic growth is thanks to its fortunate geographical position. Located near oil and gas reserves and surrounded by a vast sea line, Norway has become a hub for oil, gas, hydropower and seafood. Being so closely located to much of Europe, Norway has been able to achieve monopoly, especially in the European market in all those industries.

Naturally, as the country's wealth grew, the means to create more resources and opportunities for football has also increased. For years Norway's harsh climate meant football wasn't always accessible to young kids during the cold winter months. It is why hockey has historically dominated as the country's number one sport. But with the growth in prosperity that landscape has changed, and pitches have been built that can host players even during the coldest weather.

This means that at grassroots level there are more venues and opportunities for young Norwegians to play their beloved sport. The Norwegian Football Federation (NFF) has also introduced a player development model for young players aged 12 to 16. In that age group, potential talents are regularly monitored and analysed at a local level to work out a methodical selection process for the youth national teams. In turn, the NFF is also continuing to invest in coaches, creating programs to ensure every grassroots football club has at least some qualification that is fit for the role. This forward-thinking approach is undoubtedly contributing to a resurgence in Norwegian football.

But the past cannot be forgotten. The rise of trailblazing talents like Ole Gunnar Solskjær has also helped to increase the level of scouting in the region. Players like Erling Haaland and Martin Ødegaard were regularly monitored from a young age by the best clubs in world football. The likes of Manchester United, Arsenal and Liverpool all followed them extensively. Ødegaard was even invited on a trial at Liverpool. Meanwhile, scouts from Manchester United watched Haaland but decided against pursuing a move.

The increased level of scouting in the country has put Norwegian players in the mainstream. It has given them the ability to showcase their talent in front of the watching eyes of scouts from some of the biggest clubs in the world.

There are still some barriers to overcome in terms of profiling. One of the reasons why Haaland was rejected was because many Premier League clubs viewed him as a traditional target man, the typical type of forward Norway produced during the 1990s and early 2000s. But Norway have come a long way from being recognised as merely a hardworking, physically strong team – essentially a hockey team on grass.

The NFF's development model concentrates on technique and skill acquisition on game-based learning. There is now much more emphasiss on individual training focused on each position to bring the best out of a certain player. This has led to Norway creating different types of players compared to the past.

The likes of Ødegaard, with his brilliant technique, do not fit into the previously conventional and archaic stereotypical description of a Norwegian footballer. Neither does Haaland, with his speed and power, but also his excellent technique, which makes it so impossible for defenders to thwart him in his tracks.

'We are now creating different types of players, not just the typical hardworking Norwegian, but technical players like Ødegaard and physical players like Haaland and [Sander] Berge,' said Vik.

The level of increased investment has also created added competition at a domestic level. Up until the 2020/21 season Norwegian clubs hadn't been able to get past the last 32 in the Champions League or Europa League, or its predecessor the UEFA Cup, since they had begun to compete in European football.

But in 2021, Molde made it to the last 16 in the Europa League for the first time in Norwegian history. The following season, FK Bodø/Glimt went even better, in achieving a quarter-final finish in European football for the first time, before ultimately being eliminated by AS Roma – the eventual champions – in the Europa Conference League.

These are significant achievements, and all are pointing towards a positive change in Norwegian football. A change that could create a golden generation and even better the success of the team of stars from the 1990s.

There are still problems to solve. Norway may have players good enough to compete against the best in international football. However, having a successful team means turning those individuals into a successful and cohesive unit.

Vik said, 'The question is, of course, how do you now fit those guys in? The national team coach needs to build the team around the star players, and I think that's when Norway will be successful. It's not that simple as now saying Norway will automatically have a great team. It has to be moulded together. The job of a national team coach is not easy.'

Norway's greatest achievement to date has been making it out of the group stage at the 1998 World Cup. With the emergence of Haaland and Ødegaard, the ingredients are definitely there to surpass that success and end Norway's two-decade-long hiatus in a major international tournament.

# 9

# The Gambia

THE CLOCK was ticking. It was now or never. As Gambia surged up the pitch against Tunisia, Tom Saintfiet's men knew they had one last chance to do something special, to write themselves in the history books.

With the game in added time, Musa Barrow floated the ball into the Tunisian penalty area. Giant defenders leapt to clear it but none of them could. Instead, the ball fell on the chest of Ablie Jallow. Standing at 5ft 5in tall, the diminutive attacker found himself unopposed with acres of space ahead of him. He had time to control the ball, and then like a bullet he sent it flying into the back of the net – past the helpless Tunisian goalkeeper who stood frozen in time.

The players exploded into a frenzy on the pitch as Jallow wheeled off to celebrate, looking up at the heavens. Saintfiet remained calm on the sidelines. But inside he knew his team had just created an indelible memory in the history of Gambian football.

The 2021 Africa Cup of Nations was Gambia's first appearance at a major tournament. The country had been trying to get there for decades. And for many decades it felt like a distant dream. Then along came Saintfiet. A Belgian, who had managed more than 20 different teams before arriving in Gambia, he had the pedigree, and the proven track record of being able to squeeze more out of his players. The fact that he had helped to secure qualification for the tournament was already a miracle in the first place.

But what Gambia were about to do went beyond even the wildest expectation.

When Jallow scored his 93rd-minute winner against Tunisia, it confirmed Gambia's qualification into the last 16 – with Saintfiet's side finishing second above Tunisia, and level on points with Mali in first place. And this would be just the beginning.

In the last 16, Gambia would go on to beat Guinea thanks to a goal from Barrow, the talismanic forward who had played in Italy's top flight for many years with Bologna and Atalanta.

Another thrilling encounter would await Gambia in the quarter-finals against hosts Cameroon. That would prove to be a step too far with Gambia losing 2-0. But while they didn't quite manage to go all the way, there was plenty to be proud of for Saintfiet and his players.

Before he took over in 2018, getting to the finals seemed like an impossible feat. The country had endured so many failed qualifications – getting to a major tournament just seemed out of Gambia's means. When Saintfiet took over, Gambia were 168th in the FIFA world rankings. They were also the sixth-lowest country in Africa – ahead of only Seychelles, São Tomé and Príncipe, Djibouti, Eritrea and Somalia.

Under Saintfiet's leadership, Gambia transformed from a team expected to be the whipping boys even in the qualifying stages of Confederation of African Football (CAF) tournaments to one capable of competing among the top ten to 15 nations in African football.

'It's crazy when you think of how Gambia is a country of only two million people,' Saintfiet told me back in 2021. 'There is a lot of talent.'

Situated in West Africa, The Gambia is wedged in the middle of Senegal. Until the country gained independence in 1965, it was a colony of the United Kingdom. Few would be able to pinpoint its exact location on a world map, but a clue lies in the fact that it is the smallest populated country in mainland Africa. Naturally, being so small geographically comes with disadvantages. The Gambia is considered one of the poorest countries in Africa.

Many of its inhabitants flee to neighbouring Senegal or embark on a more harrowing journey to Europe in search of a better life. Football in this environment is often a place of refuge away from poverty and an escape route.

'My time there was very tough,' Alasana Manneh, a Gambian international who represented Barcelona at youth level, recalled of his upbringing in the country. 'Everyone's dream was to move abroad. We all want to help our families and we do not just play for ourselves but for them too. So, it was tough at the beginning.'

Like in most impoverished countries, many Gambian children play on the streets, and one of the nation's favourite pastimes is football.

Introduced by the British during the early 20th century, football has remained an important part of Gambian culture ever since, and despite little success at international level the country has produced superstars like Sevilla legend Biri Biri.

'It's very much a footballing country,' Saintfiet said. 'The country has always had good players. But in the last ten to 20 years the group of players playing abroad is getting bigger and bigger.'

The factors behind this growth are very much to do with both migration and increased scouting in the region. The Gambia may have a small population estimated to be around 2.35 million, but it is estimated that there are over 100,000 Gambians living abroad, either in Europe or Africa, and even more who are of Gambian origin, including Champions League-winning Liverpool defender Joe Gomez, whose father was born in the country.

According to IOM statistics from the International Organization for Migration (IOM), Gambians living abroad contribute to as much as 20 per cent of the country's GDP. With these changes, The Gambia's expats have helped to improve the country's economic standing. In the early 2000s, The Gambia's GDP was less than half a billion pounds. However, in 2024 that estimate is now close to £2bn.

This change is reflected in football as well. There are over 100 Gambians playing in European leagues – many of whom fled the country as refugees, including most notably the likes of Ebrima Darboe (who played for AS Roma) and Bakery Jatta (who played for Hamburg).

Compare that number to The Gambia's neighbour, Senegal, which, it is estimated, has around 200 professionals playing in Europe, but has a population of 16 million, almost eight times the size of The Gambia – and it becomes an even more impressive figure.

The Gambia Football Federation is also continuously seeking out European-born players who have eligibility to represent the country. Former Manchester United and Celtic defender Saidy Janko was one who was recruited. Noah Sonko Sundberg and Jesper Ceesay – both born in Sweden – are two others.

The make-up of the national team represents this change in demographics with a mixture of Gambian-born players, refugees and European-born players in the squad.

'Some were born in Gambia and bought by European teams at a young age. Others are born in Europe and some are refugees. We had a very diverse group. And it's a fantastic country. A football-loving country,' Saintfiet said.

It's also a young squad with an average age of just 25.8 years and the team is regularly filled with players under the age of 23 years old.

'We do have a few players who are in their 30s,' Saintfiet said. 'But the majority of our players are really young players. Some of them made their debuts for the national team before they even played first-team football at club level.'

All of this and the national team's achievements since Saintfiet took over paints a very bright future ahead for Gambia. But things were not always as bright.

In the five years from 2013 before Saintfiet took over, Gambia had not won one competitive match. Far from being perennial underdogs, they were simply footballing minnows.

'Even in the ten years before that, Gambia had only won nine matches in total,' Saintfiet said.

'In the beginning nobody wanted to watch the national team because they said we always lose,' Alasana Manneh remembered. 'Now everyone is focusing on us, and we are just very motivated.'

Sadibou Kamaso, who worked in the Gambia Football Federation for many years, remembered a completely different footballing landscape while he was growing up in the 1990s, 'Back in those days most of these parents didn't see football as something that was going to transform a child's life. They saw football as just a sport because most of the people who were involved in the sport at the time were doing it for their love of football and maybe to fly the country's name high.

'Club football and the like wasn't very popular. We had a few individuals who would invest their resources into clubs, but they were not even getting enough resources to be able to sustain those clubs.

'So as a young lad back here, football was seen as a sport you did mostly just for the sake of doing it, because there were no revenues and people weren't making money out of it.'

But during the beginning of the early 2010s, there had been a big shift in Gambian football. Everything began when the country qualified for the under-20 World Cup for the first time, in 2007.

It was a miraculous achievement. Gambia managed to beat Portugal and New Zealand in the group stage and thus qualified for the last 16. In the end, they were defeated at that hurdle by Austria – but the team's performance in that tournament attracted the attention of the footballing world.

For the first time there was an influx of players moving abroad from The Gambia. The best performers from the tournament earned moves to European and North American clubs. It was the beginning of a snowball effect – one that has gradually helped the game evolve to unprecedented heights in the subsequent decades.

'In the last sort of ten or 15 years that's kind of shifted,' Kamaso explained. 'You have a lot more players doing well. I think Gambian teams are getting more popular as well in the domestic level.'

As those players from the under-20 World Cup started to make their mark overseas, perceptions around football started to change as well. The next generation of players following suit were the likes of Modou Barrow and Omar Colley – who paved the way even further by playing in the Premier League and Serie A with Swansea City and Sampdoria respectively.

'That's when things started to really change,' Kamaso said. 'Everyone started to realise that these people are actually gaining prominence and are making decent money. The clubs they left were also now getting some form of transfer fees and the mindset started switching from OK, this is not just a game to this is a sport business.'

In the country's evolution the next step was the emergence of an even more promising generation. The Musa Barrow, Alasana Manneh and Ebrima Colley generation. These players were signed directly from Gambia by elite clubs in Europe. Barrow and Colley were snapped up by Atalanta while Manneh ended up moving to Barcelona and learned his trade at the club's renowned La Masia academy.

Kamaso said, 'When we started sending all these professionals abroad and they started playing outside of Gambia and then coming to play for the national team, the expectations change, suddenly we are on even ground – because they're playing against other countries where there are so many professionals as well. So, when that happened, we realised that our players can also go to the likes of Chelsea for trials, our players can also go to the likes of Atalanta and stuff like that. They can gain prominence in Europe, then people started seeing bigger and bigger transfer fees and how those players would come back to The Gambia and change the lives of their families, the lives of the community that they live in. That's when everything started to shift even more.'

Inspired by the generations that have come before, more and more children have taken up football. As a result, investment into the sport has grown as well, and the Gambian top flight has also become more competitive.

'At grassroots level everyone plays football in regional areas,' Saintfiet said. 'And there are professional leagues ruhn by the FA.'

By the mid-2020s, The Gambia has become a place that attracts some of the top scouts in world football. In the past, the best Gambian players would try to go to Senegal to be spotted, but since the 2010s that has become unnecessary.

'The focus of scouting is increasing in smaller countries like Gambia. Years ago, everyone went to big countries such as Nigeria and Ghana,' Saintfiet explained. 'But the interest is increasing in smaller countries as well and that gives younger players opportunities.'

Italian football intermediary Luigi Sorrentino, who visited The Gambia on numerous occasions and spotted players like Musa Barrow and Ebrima Colley, agreed, 'I like to visit the country and work with Gambian players. The Gambian players, they like to work. All my Gambian players like to work a lot. I love their attitude.'

Those three previous generations, starting from the under-20 World Cup in 2007, have created an environment where aspiring young players have more attention, more resources and more eyes on them.

With added resources, Gambia have gone on to achieve even more success following on from that under-20 World Cup in 2007. In 2021 they finished third at the under-20 AFCON, even beating eventual champions Ghana in the group stage.

Two years later they went one better, losing out to Senegal in the final of the competition. In that same year Gambia topped a group with France, South Korea and Honduras at the under-20 World Cup, and were only knocked out by winners Uruguay in the last 16.

Spearheading Gambia's under-20 side during both AFCON and the World Cup in 2023 was Abdoulie Bojang, former player turned coach with years of experience coaching within the country.

'Looking at the teams that we've played against, these are big footballing nations when it comes to finance infrastructure, I think they're way ahead of us,' Bojang reflected back on the tournament.

'We managed to beat France – which was a very big moment for us. It just shows that football is played on the pitch and during the course of the 90 minutes anything can happen.'

Only 45 years old at the time of the 2023 under-20 World Cup, Bojang was a young coach with fresh ideas. And he created a tactically astute exciting team that fought fiercely on the pitch, very much in the spirit of Saintfiet's senior side at the 2021 AFCON.

'The most important thing when you are on the pitch, when you step up in the field is to try to execute exactly what you train,' Bojang said.

'That is the secret weapon we use to win games. If you have personal confidence in yourself and you try to dominate the games, you can win against any other team. We've seen so many upsets during competitions. For me my personal belief is a team can be better than you on paper, but it has to be proven during the 90 minutes and in those 90 minutes anything is possible. Nothing is played on paper. What happens on the pitch is the most important and that's in your control.'

While Gambia's success in the under-20 AFCON in 2021 was impressive, the next generation in 2023 under Bojang hit an even higher level, and showed the exciting new face of the country's football. These were young players who were full of confidence, and who truly believed in their abilities. Sixteen years on from Gambia's first appearance at the tournament, their success beating France and only narrowly losing to the champions shows just how far they have come in the last decade and a half.

They've also inspired yet another new generation coming through. Their games were broadcast on local television networks, and the whole country tuned in to watch the matches live.

Bojang, who also worked in a local academy when he was not fulfilling his duties with the national team, remembered how children in their dozens flocked to join his club upon his return. All of them had been inspired and determined to follow suit of the under-20 stars.

He said, 'You know it made so many people come to join the academy. We could not accommodate them all because we have a number to work with. They were all excited. I remember they were telling me, "We wanted to play for the national team, we want to play for the under-20s." I tell them just take their time, keep working all the time, and when the right time comes to take their chances. That is what is important when it comes to development.

'But definitely they are all excited and it gives them added motivation and encourages them to keep working hard, so that one day they can also become footballers and call this their profession.'

Many of the stars of the under-20 team moved on to European clubs, including Adama Bojang, who was on the radar of Liverpool, Manchester United and many other top clubs – again showing how far the level of scouting has evolved. Previously, players like Bojang wouldn't even be under consideration at the best clubs in England, and Europe. In the end he decided to sign for Reims in Ligue 1 – in favour of the promise of regular first-team football.

'Adama is a very disciplined player and he's hard-working. He's always willing to learn, he listens to people, he will take advice. Definitely, he loves the game. He's determined all the time. And he will find time to do extra work and things like that. He's worked very hard to achieve whatever he has achieved so far,' Bojang, who is the uncle of Adama, said.

At senior level Saintfiet always placed a key emphasis on getting more young players involved in the setup. During his reign the likes of Yankuba Minteh, Musa Barrow, Ablie Jallow and many others made their debuts before they were even 21 years old.

'There will be sometimes mistakes made by the younger players, but that's part of the process. As a player and as a coach you learn from that and as a result you become stronger,' said Saintfiet.

Despite having a young side, Saintfiet didn't just make history helping Gambia qualify for their first AFCON tournament. He also guided the national team to two subsequent appearances, taking Gambia to the 2023 finals as well.

One of the key factors behind Saintfiet's success has been the fact that he made Gambia extremely difficult to beat by deploying quick, counterattacking football. It didn't always make him the most popular coach in the country, but it made his side extremely efficient, and you cannot argue with the results.

'When you build a house, you need good foundations and a strong structure, so that's how I approached it. When I came to Gambia my first goal was to stop conceding goals,' he explained.

'I have a lot of experience in coaching organisation and counterattacking football. So I set up the same way in Gambia. Naturally the players adapted very fast to that. The instant success gave us more confidence in the tactics too. It was like a snowball effect.'

During the early stages, giants like Algeria were unable to beat Saintfiet's resilient Scorpions on two occasions during their qualifying games for the 2019 AFCON, which they would go on to win. But there were others who struggled as well, and ultimately it was because of Saintfiet's strong defensive tactics – conceding just seven goals in qualifying – that his side were able to qualify for the 2021 AFCON. In that same year, Saintfiet's men went on a run of nine games where they were defeated just once and won five times.

Saintfiet said, 'A lot of teams would like to play like Barcelona, but they don't have the players for that. At the end of the day, it's the result that counts. I think about 80 per cent of our goals are scored in the second half, and we score many times in the transition sequences. That's our quality, going very fast in the transitions, using our speed on the wings and the idea of our system is concentrated on not losing unnecessary energy during the match. We try to make a difference at the end of the match.'

In total under Saintfiet, Gambia won a remarkable 18 games in six years – more than had been won in the previous decade before his arrival. His team lost just 16 times in 43 matches – which makes Saintfiet the most successful manager in Gambia's history.

With more and more players having gone abroad, the potential is enormous and Saintfiet set some ambitious targets for the country when we spoke in 2021.

'I think the target has to be the 2026 World Cup,' Saintfiet said. 'For many reasons. The first reason is that in that tournament not five but nine African countries will qualify. The second reason is because our very young players who are between 18 and 22 years old will be in their prime.

'I really believe that with the quality The Gambia have and knowing that they are going to improve even more, and with our young players growing in experience, the country has a good chance to do very well and make the World Cup.'

Perspectives have well and truly shifted in Gambia football. Football has become a place of celebration and joy. Alasana Manneh can testify to that as well.

'It's crazy after we win a game, it's always like we win a final in the dressing room,' Manneh said. 'It's not easy for us to come together. We only have a few games in a year so when we win everybody goes mental. The whole country. The players. Everyone. We are all happy.

'It wasn't always like this but now we win every game after each other and this is what we would like to continue. We try to make the country proud.'

Whereas years ago few people were excited by the prospect of the sport in the country, now Gambia has well and truly been stuck by football fervour. In the coming years that fervour will only continue to spread.

# 10

# Georgia

FOR A brief flicker, Nika Kvekveskiri stuttered, but then he ran forward in full flow and stabbed the ball past the outstretched hands of Greece's Odysseas Vlachodimos.

In that exact moment, as Kvekveskiri's shot hit the back of the net, around him the Georgian crowd roared in delight. Fans embraced each other in the stands and stormed the pitch. On the streets of Tbilisi, traffic stood still and car horns echoed around the ambient night.

Tuesday, 26 March 2024 will be a date for ever etched in Georgian folklore as the day the country made history: the day Georgia's football team finally qualified for a major tournament as an independent nation.

It had been decades in the making.

From 1922 until 1991, Georgian football (and Georgian society as a whole) had been suppressed by the Soviet Union. During those years Georgia was part of a myriad of countries that made up the Soviet Union. Under its tight grip, Georgian football clubs and players had to compete for the Soviet Union rather than their own nation.

The country's best stars had to represent the Soviet Union at major international tournaments and there was a concentrated effort to quell all forms of national identity. When Georgia's most successful club, Dinamo Tbilisi, won the UEFA Cup Winners' Cup back in 1981, it was celebrated as a success for the Soviet Union, rather than for Georgia.

All of that changed when the Soviet Union collapsed, and Georgia voted for independence in a referendum on 9 April 1991.

In the subsequent decade, Georgia produced plenty of talented footballers, from Georgi Kinkladze, who turned heads left, right and centre while playing in the Premier League for Manchester City, to AC Milan's Kakha Kaladze, who won the Champions League, and Shota Arveladze, who was a prolific goalscorer and played for Rangers and Ajax at the peak of his career.

What Georgia lacked during the first couple of decades of independence was funding and a cohesive and competitive environment. These players may have flourished, but in general Georgia's national team were poor, and the standards of the domestic league were relatively subpar as well.

Between 2000 and 2016, Georgia had finished bottom or second from bottom in their qualifying group for the European Championship or the World Cup on five different occasions. In that same period no Georgian team had qualified for the group stages of either the Champions League or the Europa League.

The post-Soviet Union era had brought its financial difficulties and that seeped into football. Investment had been difficult to procure.

'In the mid-'90s, the competition when we already started to form our own Georgian division was already getting weaker and weaker because the only good side in Georgia was Dinamo Tbilisi. All the other ones were so weak that for Dinamo it didn't make sense to compete with them,' Dinamo Tbilisi scout Mikha Gabechava recalled.

From the 1990s to the early 2000s, Georgian football stagnated and had been left to rot. Even with players like

Kinkladze playing really well in the Premier League, or Arveladze catching the eye for Ajax, their presence alone was not enough to compensate for the gulf in class between Georgia and their opponents at elite international level.

All of that was about to change during the beginning of the 2010s, when Georgian football would find its saviour in Andrés Carrasco. The Spaniard had worked at Barcelona's La Masia academy for over a decade. During his time with the Spanish club, he had seen the rise of players like Lionel Messi, Xavi and Andrés Iniesta. But in 2011 he sought a new challenge, and he found what he was looking for in Georgia – more specifically, Dinamo Tbilisi.

'I was looking for an adventure outside of Spain and I came to Dinamo,' Carrasco explained to me back in 2022.

In Dinamo Tbilisi, Carrasco saw untapped potential and wanted to create a lifelong legacy, not just at the club but in Georgian football as well. It was the opportunity to do what had never been done before at any elite Georgian club.

'Dinamo didn't have an academy when I came. We started from zero. We didn't have facilities and we didn't have coaches, so we started building from day one,' he said.

To get to where he wanted to be, Carrasco brought in his own people. He was determined to be hands-on and very involved from the beginning. He was also eager to squeeze out every bit of potential, and in his mind that meant playing the kind of attractive football which provided the fundamental basics for the education of the likes of Messi, Xabi and Iniesta at La Masia.

Carrasco said he worked with the coaches to create a style and methodology, which meant playing a 4-3-3 system, focused on keeping possession of the ball and playing out from the back. The key principles were pretty much identical to what he had learned in Barcelona.

Carrasco continued, 'We started training very similar to what we were developing in Barcelona, not only training but game style as well. With small differences, of course, because the Georgian player is not the same player as the Spanish player. But our goal has always been to try to play good football you can enjoy watching.'

Carrasco's impact at Dinamo Tbilisi was immediate. He initially spent just over a year at the club, but he transformed the academy's foundations and instilled a playing style that has become synonymous with Dinamo.

'When he [Carrasco] started working, we didn't have a lot of educated people in Georgian football, which was a huge problem. You would only see ex-players working in the Georgian Football Federation and on the higher levels of management and football,' Mikha Gabechava said.

Carrasco's presence at Dinamo changed all of that. He brought people in with new ways of thinking and gave the club a new lease of life.

Gabechava continued, 'Andrés Carrasco's experience from Spain and especially from Barcelona, I think helped us to shape our identity. What you see nowadays is that all the youth teams, from academy, the B team and the first team play the same football. So the same principle, same identity, same philosophy, which is great. This is something that doesn't happen in a lot of clubs in Georgia.

'At Dinamo when you are being promoted from one team to another and then eventually to the first team, that transition is smooth. And I believe this is because of Carrasco.'

Even after Carrasco had left Dinamo Tbilisi in 2012, the principles he established remained the same, which was why when he returned to the club a decade later, Carrasco found that the coaches he had brought in were still there, and the team was still playing the same football he had introduced.

'We have a strong identity,' Carrasco said. 'And that's why players know how to play and they know what they want, and our training and methodology is focused on this type of development.'

In the decade since Carrasco had first arrived at Dinamo Tbilisi, Georgian football had grown tremendously. When Carrasco left in 2012, Georgia were ranked 97th in the FIFA rankings. By 2023, they had risen by 20 places to 77th.

In that time, academy graduates have gone on to sign for the likes of Napoli, Valencia, Bayern Munich, Porto and Basel and regularly compete for Champions League and Europa League clubs.

One of Carrasco's biggest achievements came in discovering the country's biggest footballing star in the 21st century to date, Khvicha Kvaratskhelia. He spotted the then scrawny kid in a trial match during his first few months in Georgia. Back then not everyone was convinced by the young boy, but Carrasco saw potential, and invited Kvaratskhelia to the club's academy.

Carrasco recalled, 'He was ten years old when he came to the club. I remember that day when we were watching him play. I remember some coaches were having doubts about him. There were some who believed that he won't progress. But I saw something in him and so we signed him eventually.'

Carrasco, who had seen a fair share of young players come through the ranks at La Masia, would be proven right. Over the years Kvaratskhelia continued to develop in the Dinamo system and quickly became a sensation.

'The guy came through our whole system from the very beginning,' Carrasco continued. 'The first time I saw him, he looked quite similar to how he does now, that's the great thing about these types of players. It was the same with Messi, he looked the same when he was young that he looks now in the way that he plays. He was breaking defenders like now and doing the same things. When he was competing against the same age and one year older, and he was beating players all the time, he was brave in one vs one and he had that smartness to find the pass no one could see. He was always very skinny and looking like he could disassemble at any moment, but he made it very difficult for the defenders.'

Kvaratskhelia also had a support system behind him that allowed him to flourish, not only at Dinamo Tbilisi but in his family home as well.

'Our environment was crucial for him, but also his father is football-mad. When a player like this comes into your environment and a father who knows what he wants for his son, it helps you a lot. I think that's the best, and our facilities were able to give him the best chance to develop and grow,' said Carrasco.

'He had some difficulties; it wasn't always so easy for him. I think the good thing that he had was that his family was a football family and they supported him and they always found a way to instil his personality on him and make him the brave guy he is today.'

The foundations Dinamo provided enabled Kvaratskhelia to reach the kind of heights few have achieved in Georgian football. During the 2022/23 season, he became a sensation for Napoli and even earned the nickname *Kvaradona*, after club legend Diego Maradona, the club's supporters during the Italian side's Serie A-winning season.

On the international scene, Kvaratskhelia has been the linchpin of Georgia's side. But he hasn't been the only exciting prospect to emerge from Dinamo Tbilisi. Also in his age group was Giorgi Mamardashvili, who signed directly for La Liga club Valencia in 2021 and quickly established himself as one of the most exciting young goalkeepers in European football.

'I would say, Mamardashvili's case was unique. No player before [him] had ever transferred from Georgia directly to a top-five league, let alone a top-two league, and I mean, as soon as he transferred to Valencia, he started performing immediately,' Mikha Gabechava recalled.

Others, like Giorgi Chakvetadze, who even spent a trial at Barcelona and was sold for a club-record-fee in the 21st century to Belgian side KAA Gent, have also set the example. After the successes of Mamardashvili and Kvaratskhelia, Dinamo have also been able to sell Gabriel Sigua who went to Basel in 2023, and Luka Parkadze was snapped up by Bayern Munich in 2022 on a pre-contract.

On the international scene, ever since Carrasco's revolution, Dinamo Tbilisi have pretty much provided the spine of Georgia's national team. Nine players who played in Georgia's Euro 2024 play-off victory over Greece came through Dinamo's academy. At one point the club even had 15 academy graduates in a 26-man international squad, during the March 2023 qualifiers which saw Georgia draw 1-1 with Norway.

But it's not just at senior football where Georgia have thrived and written history, thanks to Dinamo Tbilisi's academy graduates. In 2023, the country hosted the under-21 European Championship. Drawn in a tough group with Belgium, Portugal and the Netherlands, there was little expectation of Georgia, even despite being on home soil. But the young stars blew everyone away. They beat Portugal 2-0 in the first game in front of a sell-out crowd, then drew 2-2 with Belgium in the second match thanks to an 87th-minute equaliser by Giorgi Guliashvili. They went on to draw with the Netherlands 1-1 in order to secure qualification out of the group in first place.

Georgia did all of this in front of huge crowds, previously unprecedented at a youth tournament. They broke the record attendance three times in the history of the under-21 European Championship during the tournament and set the highest attendance in the subsequent quarter-final against Israel inside Tbilisi's Boris Paichadze Dinamo Arena. The sell-out crowd amounted to 44,338 in total and produced the kind of atmosphere that's never before been seen at a youth tournament hosted by UEFA.

'In the past few years, the interest around Georgian football has been rising and it's great to see because every time the national team plays, it's a sell-out. Like immediately. After a maximum of two hours the tickets are gone,' Mikha Gabechava said.

'I think people have started to realise that this generation is different and that's why they are so excited.'

While in the end Georgia bowed out at the quarter-final stage after a cruel penalty shoot-out to Israel, this was yet another example of the country's growing rise in football. Again, Dinamo's influence was clear. More than half of the players – 13 – in the squad at the tournament were Tbilisi academy graduates. Six were in the starting XI that beat Portugal 2-0 in the opening game of the tournament.

Many of those young players who competed at the under-21 tournament have then gone on to represent Georgia at senior level, including at Euro 2024.

Much of that is thanks to Andrés Carrasco's influence. The man from Barcelona had arrived and transformed the entire foundations of Georgian football. Without him it is moot whether Georgia would have been able to qualify for Euro 2024 and begin a new exciting era in the country's history.

With Khvicha Kvaratskhelia and Giorgi Mamardashvili now setting new standards and examples, and Dinamo continuing to maintain Carrasco's foundations, his legacy will endure. In the years to come more will follow in their footsteps.

# 11

# Ecuador

WHEN THE final whistle blew inside the Estadio General Pablo Rojas on 9 November 2019, Miguel Ángel Ramírez's players, wearing pink and white, exploded in jubilation. His assistant beside him was reduced to tears.

Independiente del Valle had won the Copa CONMEBOL Sudamericana for the first time, beating Argentine side Colón. A decade prior, to even dream of such success at Independiente del Valle would have been a fantasy.

The club was founded in 1958 by José Terán and some of his friends. Back then Independiente del Valle looked completely different. Terán's team wore red-and-white-striped shirts, and they were called Club Deportivo Independiente, inspired by the Argentine side CA Independiente.

For most of the club's early history, Independiente competed in the lower divisions of Ecuador, and were rarely promoted to even the third tier, let alone the top flight. Dreams of making it to the Sudamericana – which is South America's equivalent of the Europa League – seemed like a fanciful wish.

However, that all changed in 2007. Amid financial difficulties at Independiente, a wealthy businessman, Michel Deller, decided to buy the club. Deller was keen to invest in football and had lofty ambitions. He renamed the club as Independiente del Valle and changed the team's colours to black and white. Immediately, he brought in a lot of investment and sought to transform the fortunes of Independiente.

Under him, Independiente were promoted to the second division for just the second time later that year, and then in 2009 they earned a historic promotion to Ecuador's top tier for the first time.

The factors behind the club's rise can be detailed by Deller's decision to build a sustainable model. It meant focusing on youth development being at the core of the club's values and investing in young players with potential, who Independiente would later be able to sell for major profits.

After promotion, Independiente became a stable and regular member of the top flight during the following decade. They also started to produce a considerable amount of players for Ecuador's senior national team.

'In Ecuador, if you are a football coach, you want to work for Independiente del Valle. And this is the same if you want to be a footballer,' the club's former academy coach Ricardo Oquendo said.

'It's the place to be, to be honest. I don't know if [it's the same in] all the Americas because the MLS has developed a lot, but at least in South America, I'm really sure that there are not many better places than Independiente.'

Deller's focus on youth football saw Independiente build an impressive structure. The club set up a second team in the second division of Ecuadorian football, and a myriad of satellite academies and schools across the country.

The satellite schools have ensured that talents are spotted at an early age at a local level, and that Independiente maintain hegemony in scouting across the country.

'The scouting plays a very key role [in the success of Independiente],' Oquendo explained. 'It's a crucial part of the club. There is a huge network of scouts all over the country looking for potential players for the club. And the scouting department at the club is very good at what they do.'

With the establishment of the schools, Independiente's regional coaching staff often also identify potential talents as well. The best talents spotted at the regional schools are often brought into Independiente's main base at the academy and live inside the club's campus.

'With the many different academies across the country, what happens is that we bring the talents in and we train them with the same methodology of Independiente del Valle,' said Oquendo.

'They are not the club, but they are a branch of the club. And if you are a potential player, you then have the chance to be invited to the academy and become part of the club.'

Independiente's expansion across Ecuador has made the club extremely attractive to future players. It has taken Independiente from a relative minnow in Ecuadorian football back in 2007 to one of the most popular clubs in the country and a source of hope for many.

Ecuador has been stricken with poverty since the 1990s. It has been regarded as one of the poorest countries in South America. Football and Independiente have offered many of the country's children a route out of that struggle.

'Every single kid in Ecuador wants to become a footballer, which means every single kid wants to be part of the academy,' Oquendo said. 'In Ecuador it's not only about becoming a star and how many titles you are going to win [when kids dream of becoming a footballer]. But for us it's not just about success. If you understand Ecuadorian context, we are a poor country in financial terms; 99 per cent of the players in the academy come from poorer areas and poor families. For them, it's not only "I want to become a footballer so I can be a star" but also "I want to become a footballer so I can help my family come out of poverty". To me I think this motivation of Ecuadorian players is very special, and very different compared to European players.'

At Independiente, everything is set up to help the players achieve that dream. The club's structure and organisation is methodically focused on bringing the best out of every player and maximising potential.

The academy is also geared towards creating natural pathways to the first team. Every team and age group follows a similar regime during the week, and each group at least partially focuses on playing styles that are used in the first team.

'In the club we had a game model based on the methodology of positional play. And this game model was taught from under-12s all the way to the first team,' Oquendo said.

All the teams train from Monday to Friday, including the younger categories. The coaches for each team have an extensive training calendar that is different each week – to focus on different areas of the game.

'From Monday to Wednesday we would train the game model based on positional play, then Thursday and Friday we trained the core pillars of the game model – which means during the first part of the week we trained the aspects of the game we thought the players were lacking and then during the second part of the week, it was more preparation for the games,' Oquendo said.

'It doesn't matter if you were under-12 or under-18, we trained the same concepts from Monday to Friday. Only the first team is a bit more different, it is more competition-oriented rather than focused on development.'

With every single player learning the core principles of the club from a young age, this means moving into the first team is made a lot easier later on. Players don't have to learn new styles and new systems; they can go from the academy to the first team and expect the same drills and same principles.

'The most important thing in the club has been from my point of view is a clear idea, a clear organisation and very clear club culture, what we want as a club and how we work as coaches. All the first-team coaches were very close to the academy coaches. Very strong culture,' added Oquendo.

The strong unity and the strong bond between academy and first team allowed Miguel Ángel Ramírez to earn a promotion from being the director of the academy to take on the role of head coach for the senior team.

Under him the club didn't just enjoy success, but also brought through some of the best young players to have played for Independiente, including the one and only Moisés Caicedo, who would later become the most expensive transfer in Premier League history during the summer of 2023. Caicedo, too, highlights the unity at the club as a key reason behind Independiente's success.

'For me [on the secret of the club] it's coherence. You do what you really believe. I mean you are coherent. You are honest, honest with yourself. You have a project. And you are loyal to this project and to this belief,' Ramírez said.

'Independiente has a strong base. They spend money, big money in the academy and they want to. The club has many scouts, many football academies and schools around the country, so they are the top one in the market in Ecuador. They get the first place detecting and finding good players in the country. So this is the first thing – the detection of the talent.'

But it's not just about what goes on in terms of spotting the talents. It's also about what Independiente provides. Deller has developed a state-of-the-art academy complex that according to Ramírez is comparable to some of the best facilities in world football. Not only does it have multiple hectares of pristine football pitches but it is also equipped with a games room, a library and a cinema.

'They spend a lot of money to have good facilities. They have the school. They have good food and good pitches to train on,' said Ramírez.

To keep the players in check, Independiente also provide elite coaches and educators who nurture the club's young stars.

Ramírez explained, 'The club puts a strong emphasis in the education of the coaches, because if you want good players, you need good coaches. So, we spent too many hours helping the coaches to better understand the game, to prepare better the training sessions. The exercises, "Why this exercise? Why not that?" We explain everything to them. Then we have many meetings during the week to follow up the processes and evaluate the processes. And evaluate every six months, every single player, and we talk about every single player every six months to evaluate them in all terms of psychology, technically, tactically, physically. So, the club has a strong and serious project. And they have good professionals to perform this project.'

Since winning the Sudamericana under Ramírez, Independiente have also lifted the league title in Ecuador for the first time, in 2021, and won the Sudamericana once again, in 2022. Success, though, is really measured by the amount of academy graduates who have gone on to play at the highest level in Europe.

The record-breaking Caicedo is just one name among the myriad of stars who have gone on to excel in Europe and become a key part of Ecuador's national team. The list includes the likes of Piero Hincapié, Ángelo Preciado, Gonzalo Plata and Willian Pacho.

'For me the importance of Independiente is the key not only for Caicedo, but for all the other guys that are growing now and showing up in the top places like in Hincapié or Pacho or Preciado, all these young boys,' Ramírez said.

'A flower can't grow on asphalt. A flower needs good ground and water and you need to take care of the flower to get a good one. So, of course, they [academy players] have the talent but without Independiente it would have been much more difficult. Independiente worked and developed their talents and helped them grow. Independiente gave the tools and provided the good environment to develop these tools and it was the key to help in their development.'

In the Ecuador squad for the 2022 World Cup, nine members came through the ranks at Independiente – by far the most out of any other Ecuadorian club. An additional two members also became established stars while playing for Independiente and earned moves abroad using the club as a springboard to build their careers.

Impressively, in Qatar, Ecuador also boasted the third-youngest team at the tournament behind the United States and Ghana with an average age of just 25.6 years old. Most of the nine Independiente graduates hadn't even turned 23 years old at the time of the finals.

This was only a sign of things to come. In that same year, another young player emerged at Independiente, who has broken records set by the likes of Diego Maradona, and who has excited many inside the country: Kendry Páez.

Ricardo Oquendo has known him for years, having been his coach at under-12 level.

'He was my best player. He was amazing, this is a guy who is totally outstanding in all the conditions. Technically he is amazing, and then his positional understanding is something else as well. When he was with me at under-12 level, we already knew that this kid would not only become a professional but that he would play in Europe as well,' Oquendo said.

At 16 years old Páez became the youngest Ecuadorian to debut in the senior national team, and the youngest to score as well. When he made his debut he became the second-youngest South American to play for his country, with Diego Maradona holding that distinction. However, when Páez scored for Ecuador against Bolivia in a World Cup qualifier, he beat out all the South American superstars who came before him, becoming the youngest player ever to score in CONMEBOL qualifying.

At such a young age, Páez's emergence into the senior game has been unprecedented in Ecuadorian football. Chelsea acted quickly during the summer of 2023, tying the youngster down on a pre-contract.

Oquendo had full faith in Páez, and believed he represented the ideal player for Independiente, 'He was a match-winner. I remember a free kick outside or close to the box, we celebrated it like it was a goal because we knew he was going to score. He is the perfect model for the academy. The kind of player we want to bring through all the time.'

It's obvious that Páez will not be the last player to come through Independiente's ranks. Thanks to the club's impressive track record over the last decade and a half, Ecuadorian football has risen in stature. Evidence can also be found in Ecuador's performances at youth tournaments since Independiente emerged as a major force inside the country.

In 2019, Ecuador won the under-20 Copa América. That same year they also finished third at the under-20 World Cup, beating the likes of Italy, Uruguay and the

United States en route to that achievement. Four years later the country's young stars also qualified for the under-20 World Cup, and were narrowly eliminated in the last 16.

At under-17 level Ecuador also reached the last 16 at the World Cup in 2019 and 2023, and finished fourth at the under-17 Copa América in 2019, before ending up as the runners-up in 2023.

At the senior World Cup, Ecuador's best achievement to date was in 2006, when they made it out of the group stage after finishing second behind hosts Germany before ultimately being eliminated by England in the last 16.

For several years, surpassing that achievement seemed impossible but, with Independiente del Valle's work, Ecuadorian football has entered a new realm, and the limits are boundless.

# 12

# Hungary

ON 25 November 1953, the crowd of more than 100,000 crammed into Wembley Stadium witnessed what no English fan had witnessed in over 80 years – defeat at home. At the time England were considered unbeatable on their own grounds. Yet along came a ragtag team from the Eastern Bloc who blew the hosts away.

The Hungarian team, or 'Mighty Magyars' as they were later called, were not a new sensation. They had an unbeaten run of their own, and were Olympic champions in 1952. Managed by Gusztáv Sebes, they played an innovative style of football that was more in line with the modern game at the time.

But few expected them to break England's long-standing record. Even the visitors' biggest star, Ferenc Puskás, was a little awestruck by the prospect of facing England as he later admitted in his autobiography published in 1955.

'All these results made me sick,' Puskás recalled. 'The British press referred to the fixture as the match of the century. Some sarcastic remarks were made about us in some newspapers, which meant that England was feeling as confident as possible.'

Those nerves definitely didn't show in the way Hungary swept aside England. Playing with rigour and a possession-based system that England had no idea how to combat, Hungary played the home team's superstars off the park.

The 'Game of the Century', as it would be dubbed, proved the crowning moment of a golden era in Hungarian football. Soon it would be about to experience a colossal collapse beginning with defeat to West Germany in the 1954 World Cup Final and then doomed by the 1956 Hungarian revolution. The horrific events which unfolded as the Soviet Union suppressed the Hungarian people's revolt against the strict communist regime ultimately and very prematurely cut an end to the greatest Hungarian side in history. Having witnessed the events from afar, the country's top stars such as Puskás decided to flee and defect to the west, which saw them subsequently banned from playing for the national team.

They ended up playing for the biggest clubs in world football. Puskás signed for Real Madrid and won the European Cup three times with the Spanish giants, scoring four goals in one final – he is still the player to have scored the most goals in European Cup and World Cup finals. Sándor Kocsis and Zoltán Czibor moved to Barcelona to form a golden trio with another Hungarian at the club, László Kubala.

All four of them enjoyed tremendous success during their careers in Spain, but in Hungary they were labelled as traitors to the communist regime and their achievements would only be discovered later.

With Hungary's team dismantled, and no longer an effective propaganda tool for the communist government, naturally interest and funding waned from the regime. The 1960s, and more precisely the 1970s, saw the decline of football. When the communist regime eventually collapsed in 1989, the economic downfall saw the sport even more neglected during the 1990s. That is reflected in the fact that between 1986 and 2016, Hungary did not qualify for a single major tournament. The 30-year exile saw Hungary turn from a stalwart European footballing nation to a minnow.

However, as the impact of communism and its downfall eased, during the beginning of the 21st century Hungary started to make a concentrated effort to return to that previous golden era. At the forefront of these developments has been one of the country's most historic clubs, MTK Budapest.

In 2001, MTK became the first Hungarian club to establish an elite football academy. Named after club legend Károly Sándor, the academy has played a pivotal role in the rise of Hungarian football over the course of the early 2020s.

'Everything is built at this club to develop and produce players,' Zsolt Székely, who is MTK's academy director and has worked at the academy since its foundation, said. 'It's simply part of our DNA. From the cleaning staff to the academy coaches, everyone shares our philosophy.

'Ever since I could remember, everyone [in Hungary] had been saying how important academy football was and how we had to put everything into the development of young players but this was always just an excuse to explain why Hungarian football wasn't very good; no one actually bothered to put in the work, except for MTK.

'When the academy started in 2001, this was the only academy for five to six years. Since then, we have had some competition, but I still think in terms of player development and coaching we are the best in the country.'

The academy's first successful achievement occurred in 2006, just five years after its foundation. That year Attila Filkor, who had come through the ranks at MTK Budapest and had trials at Manchester City and Tottenham, made his debut for Inter Milan, playing for half an hour in the Coppa Italia. Only 18 years old at the time, Filkor was regarded as one of the most exciting players to have emerged from Hungary for decades. His debut was one of the most talked about Hungarian footballing achievements that year. Renowned Hungarian journalist György Szöllősi dubbed this as the *Filkorszak*, which can be translated to the 'Filkor era', and used it to highlight how far Hungary had fallen from their old prestige. A nation that once proudly beat England at Wembley now celebrated one player making a brief cameo in the early rounds of the Coppa Italia as its crowning footballing achievement in the calendar year.

Filkor never fulfilled the hype that surrounded him. He didn't even make a single Serie A appearance for Inter Milan, and although he went on to sign for the club's rivals AC Milan, he never made a single senior appearance during his five-year stint there either. Constantly wracked by injuries, he played most of his career in Serie B before returning to Hungary and retiring at the age of 34 with just six senior national team appearances under his name.

However, the Filkor phenomenon proved to be a catalyst for Hungarian football. In 2008, at the under-19 European Championship, a Hungary team made up of MTK graduates reached the semi-finals.

It was a tournament that boasted the likes of Toni Kroos, Jordi Alba and Daniel Sturridge, yet so impressive was the Hungarian squad that four players were named in the Team of the Tournament including Péter Gulácsi and Krisztián Németh.

By then Gulácsi and Németh, both of whom came through the ranks at MTK Budapest, were Liverpool players. In 2007, on the back of an impressive showing at the previous year's under-17 European Championship, Liverpool struck a partnership with MTK Budapest which saw Gulácsi, Németh and András Simon join the English giants' academy.

At the time Liverpool manager Rafael Benítez and the club's chief scout, Frank McParland, sought to broaden the Reds' academy recruitment and recognised potential in MTK Budapest's burgeoning academy.

'It was an interesting period. Liverpool first came for Simon. They scouted him at the national team and they really liked him. Then they also had a scout who saw that a lot of talented players come out from our academy so they came to us in Agard [where the MTK academy was based at the time], and there they also spotted Gulácsi and Németh,' Zsolt Székely explained.

'We then signed a partnership where they helped to support the academy and they also had observers in the academy who spotted potential talents and brought them over to Liverpool for trials.'

On top of that, Székely also regularly travelled to England to learn from the likes of Steve Cooper at Liverpool's academy. Later, he had the opportunity to coach at Oldham Athletic through the Reds' network – with Benítez's side signing a partnership with the then League One club to bring in even more Hungarian talent and test them in the English game.

The partnership would last for six years, and it would see a plethora of young talent sign contracts with Liverpool – with varying degrees of success. While none of the players ever made it to the first team, the level of exposure and experience provided by Liverpool for coaches like Székely meant that MTK's partnership was a resounding success from the Hungarian perspective. It allowed the scouting world to take notice of Hungary and made MTK a recognised name in youth development, not just in Europe but around the world.

This, coupled with Filkor signing for Inter Milan, led to an avalanche of interest from other European clubs looking to scout the region. In 2008, PSV Eindhoven signed Balázs Dzsudzsák from Debreceni for a lucrative fee, which was another landmark development in the growth of Hungarian football during the late 2000s in the country.

The three events combined in the space of less than two years led to the recognition in the country of the potential for football as a business.

With more money coming in, the generated revenue at clubs like MTK was invested back into the academy and helped to build new facilities. Later in the 2010s, as a new government was formed in Hungary by the Fidesz party. Their introduction of a generous tax relief scheme helped to bring in even more money to an industry which had been losing money for decades. Thanks to Fidesz, many clubs were able to develop their often dilapidated training grounds and pitches to new state-of-the-art facilities.

Around the same time, something else was also happening in Hungary's lesser-known city of Székesfehérvár. In 2007, the local club, Videoton, released a young manager in charge of their under-nine team. His name was Zsolt Szoboszlai. The reason for his departure had been due to a clash with parents over Szoboszlai's decision to run two different sessions for the under-nine team, one for the more advanced group and another for the less advanced one. Some of the parents became frustrated with Szoboszlai for putting their children in the less advanced group. With these parents being rich benefactors, Szoboszlai was instructed to put their children in the advanced group. However, he refused. Instead, he simply changed the times around for the two sessions and still trained with the same players. The parents quickly caught on and Szoboszlai left the academy.

Leaving Videoton proved to be a blessing in disguise for the former professional footballer. Szoboszlai banded together with two other footballing parents and decided to go his own way. Together the three of them built Főnix Gold academy, which would provide the crucial stepping stones for one of Hungary's greatest players in the 21st century – Zsolt's son, Dominik Szoboszlai.

Főnix Gold's facilities, on the outskirts of Székesfehérvár, included a dilapidated-looking building from the outside, surrounded by the factory district. Inside, it was home to just two astroturf seven-a-side pitches, and it was where Dominik Szoboszlai spent most of his childhood.

'As soon as Dominik started to walk, he was given a ball,' Zsolt recalled of his son. 'He'd come watch my games and he seemed to have fun with it.'

When the young boy wasn't in school, he'd be out practising on the training pitch, trying to improve his game and impress his father.

'He'd practise free kicks daily, about 100 or 200 times a day,' Zsolt said.

While setting up the academy, Zsolt studied some of the best in the world at how they develop young players and incorporated the ideas he deemed best. His innovative methods included giving headbands to his players in training sessions instead of bibs to force them to look up, and making them hold golf balls while teaching them to defend, so that they wouldn't pull at the opposition's shirts.

'Our concentration is on mastering the technical skills,' Zsolt said. 'The philosophy is to play football; when you have the technical skillset it's a lot more enjoyable to just play.'

With an emphasis on mastering the technical side of the game, Zsolt's academy quickly developed a growing reputation in the country. So impressive was its rise that Főnix Gold was also invited to the renowned Cordial Cup – a youth tournament held in Austria, which hosted some of the best academies in Europe.

Impressively, Zsolt's team won the cup in 2011 and 2013, beating opponents like Bayern Munich, Basel and Red Bull Salzburg in the process. The squad didn't just include Dominik Szoboszlai, but other future national team players like Kevin Csoboth and Bendegúz Bolla, as well as many others who went on to represent Hungary at youth level.

Zsolt's work was widely recognised in Hungary and he was undoubtedly a pioneer in changing the outlook of academy coaching in the country. Like MTK Budapest, Zsolt's methods concentrated on the technical aspects of the game, and focused on teaching those key principles before anything else.

Later, when Dominik Szoboszlai was spotted by Red Bull Salzburg at an under-15 national team game, in order to prepare him for joining the Austrian club when he turned 16, out of all the academies in Hungary, Zsolt chose MTK Budapest. Dominik spent just over a year with the club, but it was enough to make even Zsolt Székely take notice.

'It was a joy to watch him play. He was incredible,' Székely remembered. 'He stood out a lot in his age group. There was a game in Mattersburg where they couldn't even get the ball out of their own half. We scored five goals, it was one of the best games I have ever seen, and I remember the coach was walking off the pitch and I could hear him telling his players to not be disappointed because they had never encountered anything like this before.'

There is no doubt that Szoboszlai took Hungarian football into a new realm. At Red Bull Salzburg, he quickly established himself as one of the best players, first at the academy, then for the club's second team, Liefering, and later the first team under Jesse Marsch.

'He came to FC Red Bull Salzburg as a very young player,' Salzburg's former sporting director, Christoph Freund, recalled.

'At the time, he was full of talent and he also had a lot of self-confidence. In this age you have to learn a lot to arrive in professional football. So, the matches for our cooperations club FC Liefering helped him a lot to improve his skills and also his mentality to become the player he is now.'

Szoboszlai had been on the periphery of the senior national squad since the age of 16. He earned his first call-up at just 17 under Bernd Storck, but in the end it was under Marco Rossi that Szoboszlai made his senior debut.

'It has been interesting to watch him grow and moving from different clubs. We had been following him from a young age,' Rossi said.

Under Rossi's guidance, Szoboszlai has grown into a leading figure in the national team. At just 20 years old he scored a last-gasp winning goal in a play-off victory against Iceland to help his country qualify for the European Championship in 2020.

Two years later, at just 22 years old, Szoboszlai was made the captain, becoming one of the youngest players to ever wear the armband in Hungary's history.

'The reason [to select him as captain] was because of his personality,' Rossi explained. 'Because of his natural leadership. And then, of course, the captain of the national team must be a role model as well. I think this decision has also accelerated his process of growing up. He is much more responsible now and he is taking things in an even more serious way than before.'

Having someone like Szoboszlai in the team has elevated the rest of the squad as well according to Callum Styles, who was among the handful of players of Hungarian descent that the country's football federation has worked extensively to bring to the national setup.

'He's a top, top player. He shows it on and off the pitch,' Styles said. 'Just to take a little bit out of his book and to implement it into our game is what we want to do and it just shows having such a good player, it lifts the whole team up. It gives us energy. It's just a blessing to have him in the team and as captain as well.'

Many in his home country regard Szoboszlai as in the realm of Puskás, and just like the former Real Madrid legend, the Liverpool midfielder has too has delivered historic results on English soil.

In 2022, Hungary managed to trump the Mighty Magyars' result in England, beating Gareth Southgate's Three Lions 4-0 in a UEFA Nations League game in Wolverhampton, which ignited a football fervour in the country.

But this achievement didn't happen thanks to Szoboszlai alone. Without a doubt, a key man in taking Hungary to new heights has been the manager, Marco Rossi. The Italian, who had an extremely successful club career in Hungary, delivering a historic title for Budapest Honvéd, has had a transformative effect on the national team since taking charge in 2019.

Under him, Hungary have risen to unprecedented heights on the FIFA rankings, and held their own against some of the best nations in world football, including eking out draws against France and Germany at Euro 2020.

During the 2022 Nations League campaign, Hungary also beat Germany and England to finish above them in the group. In 2023, Rossi's side went an entire year unbeaten and held the European record for the longest unbeaten run at the time, while earning qualification to Euro 2024 – a third subsequent appearance at the finals since 2016.

Rossi has built a young side, with plenty of potential and room to grow.

In 2022, Zalán Vancsa became the youngest player to debut for the national team in over 100 years when he appeared against Italy. That year he also signed to the City Football Group having come through the ranks at MTK Budapest.

A year later, Milos Kerkez made his debut under Rossi. He was signed by AC Milan from Győri ETO in 2021 and went on to play for Bournemouth in the Premier League while also finishing in 19th place at the prestigious 2023 FIFA Golden Boy awards.

'I feel like it's my second home, we just keep winning which is unbelievable, that's what we all want as a team,' said Callum Styles, who was born in England but qualifies to play for Hungary because of his grandparents. 'From the players to the coaching staff we have a really good group and hopefully we can bring more success our way.'

Rossi has seen a huge transformation not just on the pitch but off it as well with more interest being generated in Hungarian football by agents and scouts from abroad.

'In the last period something changed in which especially the agents, more than the clubs, are taking a look to the Hungarians,' Rossi said.

'Previously, the general opinion was that the Hungarians, even if they were talented, were not good enough or strong from a psychological point of view to react to the adversities and things like that.

'But in the last period many of our young players playing abroad showed that this was something false or at least not completely true. I think that in the future we could have even more players playing abroad and this will be, of course, a huge advantage for me or the following coaches of the national team.'

That would only help Hungary grow even more as a nation.

Rossi continued, 'Because if you have many, many players playing in the top leagues, it is much more easy to put them together, because they are used to playing in a more advanced championship when it comes to the intensity and the tactical aspects as well. Right now the guys in our team are evolving and growing and everything is working better with the national team.'

Having failed to qualify for a World Cup for 40 years, the objective now will be to build on three successful qualification campaigns to the European Championship and make that long-sought-after qualification to the 2026 global event in North America.

If anyone can do it, it's Marco Rossi and Dominik Szoboszlai. Together they have helped to concoct a team environment that even the Mighty Magyars would have been proud of.

# 13

# Australia

ONE TOUCH. One shot. And one save. Had it gone slightly different, it could have altered the history of the World Cup, and perhaps the history of football itself.

During the dying embers of Argentina's last-16 tie against Australia in the 2022 World Cup, the ball fell to Garang Kuol inside the South Americans' penalty box. At the time Kuol was the youngest player to have debuted for Australia in the 21st century. He was also the youngest player to represent his country at the World Cup, and the youngest since 1980 to score for Australia at senior international level.

This was his moment. He turned his opponent with a sublime first touch and broke through on goal. The clock ticked on, ambling into the 96th minute of the match. Kuol struck at goal with venom and power. For a brief flicker it looked like he may have just done it.

But ultimately, the football gods had a different script in mind. Emiliano Martínez made a superb save to deny Kuol and kickstart Lionel Messi's long-awaited journey to win the World Cup.

Craig Carley, watching the moment back in Shepperton, Australia, felt a whirlwind of emotions. He'd known Kuol and his brothers since they were young kids. He'd coached them and seen them grow into senior footballers, and now one of them had just caught the eye at the biggest stage in world football.

'It didn't surprise me,' Carley recalled. 'Garang, he's just a happy-go-lucky kid. Nothing fazes him. He plays football with courage. He has absolutely no fear and to see the way he went into that game just reminded me of when he came into our senior team as a 15-year-old.'

Kuol had emigrated to Australia from South Sudan aged just one year old in 2005. Alongside his brothers, Alou and Teng, he immediately picked up the sport and joined GV Suns, where Carley had worked for many years.

Within the club's academy system, Kuol worked his way up the ranks alongside his siblings. But while Alou and Teng have gone on to have successful careers, Garang has always been the most talented of the trio.

During his development years he had risen to every challenge thrown at him, and he even thrived when thrust into a first-team environment at a young age.

Carley said, 'One memory that really sticks out to me is that we put him in that environment and he was there making a mockery of our senior players and just gliding past them like they weren't even there, you know? And some of these players are ex-professional players from over in the UK. We had one player that played Championship level and Garang's there as a young kid playing with, like I said before, with no fear and just excelling.'

That game would become the springboard for Kuol's journey to the World Cup, and later Newcastle United.

Carley continued the story, 'I remember vividly that it was a pre-season game and we played against a team called Dandenong City and there was an ex-Socceroos player, Sasa Ognenovski, who played 20-odd games for Australia. We bought Garang on for about 20 to 25 minutes at the end of the game and they had had three professional players that had just sort of stepped back from the game. One was Adrian Leijer, who was actually at Fulham in the Premier League [from 2007 to 2009] and Garang just tore him to pieces.

'After the game, I remember speaking to Sasa and saying, "Look, you know you need to get this kid into the A-League. This kid like, he needs to be in a professional environment," and they sort of just laughed at me like, you know, yeah, you know, we'll keep tabs on him.

'Before you know it, I was speaking to [manager] Nick Montgomery at Central Coast Mariners and yeah, you know the rest.'

Kuol went on to play 22 games at senior level for Central Coast Mariners, scoring seven goals and earning that call-up to the World Cup. His appearance at the tournament made him only the second-youngest player in Qatar, behind Germany's Youssoufa Moukoko.

As he slumped to the ground holding his head when the final whistle blew against Argentina, despite Australia's elimination the country and player had plenty to be proud of.

The 2022 World Cup was a hugely positive tournament for Australia, and a glimpse of a bright future ahead. Graham Arnold's men beat Denmark and Tunisia to finish second in their group and record the country's best performance at the World Cup. Australia achieved this with nine players aged 24 or younger in the squad, including Kuol, who was by far the youngest.

But it wasn't just successful on the pitch. It was also successful off it. While Australia has produced over 50 players for the Premier League, including stars like Harry Kewell and Tim Cahill, football (or soccer) has always had to compete with Australian rules football and cricket – sports that are still far more popular. The World Cup was evidence that this hegemony was changing. Approximately 1.7 million people tuned in to watch Australia's last-16 game against Argentina – which was the second-highest broadcast on Australia's SBS channel that year.

It's not only the popularity that continues to grow, but the game has been advancing in Australia as well. In 2013, the National Premier League was established in the country, which acts as a second tier, behind Australia's top level – the A-League. Divided into eight regional divisions, to accommodate for Australia's large geographical size, the leagues are made up of 90 professional and semi-professional teams.

At the moment of writing, there is no promotion for the eight regional divisions, but depending on the State Federation, some teams may be relegated to their respective third divisions.

There are also future plans to create a nationwide format that will enable promotions to the A-League, but they are yet to be formulated by the Australian Soccer Federation.

According to Carley, this change has been fundamental to the growth and development of Australian soccer, 'For me, the pathways have improved with the introduction of the National Premier League. Prior to that players were travelling down to Melbourne, which is sort of two and a half hours from us; they were doing that three or four times a week as juniors just to, you know, train and make those national youth squads or you know play for the better team in the region.

'Whereas the introduction of the NPL pathway has allowed for our coaches to be upskilled to give our players a proper football education. It has also allowed younger players to play against better opposition players and better ability without the need to travel for hours. So I think for us it has been really important.'

Prior to the National Premier League, according to Carley players like Kuol would end up travelling hours to nearby A-League teams to train in their respective academy setups.

But with the NPL, local clubs have been able to generate money and create more professional environments, allowing youngsters to have access to the same sort of coaching and competitive football that they would have at A-League clubs without the need to travel for hours every day just to be able to train.

Essentially, the NPL has given access to high-quality coaching to a wider pool of young Australian players. It has allowed clubs like Carley's Goulburn Valley Suns to pivot their strategy towards player development and create a viable income through player sales.

Players like Kuol have been one of the first generations to have fully benefitted from the system changes. But despite the NPL helping to improve Australian soccer's development system, it is far from perfect.

Clubs at NPL level charged fees to most of their academy players, payments which have often been difficult to finance, especially for players who come from underprivileged backgrounds. Kuol and his brothers belonged to those families for whom paying GV Suns' fees would have been impossible. But the club recognised their talent and found ways around Kuol and his siblings having to pay for their footballing education.

Carley explained, 'We have young players from all different backgrounds, ethnic backgrounds, you know, diverse backgrounds and the majority of our youngsters can't afford to pay the fees to play in the NPL system. So, we've sort of come up with our own method that if they're good enough to play, then they play and we'll find a way to finance that.

'I think that's why we've seen a lot of success with our juniors and certainly the Kuol kids, as an example, I truly believe that they would have been lost within the system had it not been for the club being set up the way it is. I think, you know, we could have lost them to other sports or they would just be playing local soccer, local football in the region.'

Kuol and his brothers have also been representative of the changing face of Australia and Australian soccer. In the 21st century, the country has welcomed tens of thousands of refugees per annum, many of whom were fleeing war and poverty. The Kuols fled South Sudan due to political tensions in the region, and ultimately found refuge in Australia.

They are not alone. The story of Mohamed Toure and his siblings follows a similar pattern. Born in Conakry, to a family of Liberian refugees, Toure and his family found refuge in Australia in 2004, after spending close to 14 years living in a refugee camp.

Nestory Irankunda was born in Tanzania after his family fled Burundi during the civil war in 2006. Irankunda and his family, too, found a home in Australia.

Together, Irankunda and Toure are the two youngest players to have scored in the A-League since its foundation. Toure was just 15 years, ten months and 19 days old when he netted. Meanwhile, Irankunda was 15 years, 11 months and 21 days. Kuol is the sixth-youngest, having scored at 17 years, six months and 21 days.

All three of them have made lucrative transfers to Europe. Toure moved to Ligue 1 side Reims in 2022, Kuol signed for Newcastle United in January 2023, and Irankunda completed a move to Bayern Munich in 2023.

The development of Australian football had grown stagnant since the 2010s when the likes of Harry Kewell, Mark Viduka and Tim Cahill retired from playing. But with the emergence of Kuol, Toure and Irankunda in the 2020s, a new generation has ignited hope for a resurgence.

'It's exciting times for Australian football at the moment,' Carley said.

'I think it's been a long time since Australia sort of had any talented players since the golden generation of the early 2000s. There's been a big void in players coming through, but I think now with the introduction of the NPL system, I think you'll see a lot more youngsters coming through, not only from the sort of privileged or good backgrounds but, you know, kids from all different diverse backgrounds.'

But the NPL system hasn't just created and helped to professionalise clubs across a wider region in the game, it's also created more pathways for youngsters to follow.

Since its introduction A-League clubs have regularly monitored the best up-and-coming talent, and follow the work of regional NPL teams very closely. At GV Suns, A-League side Central Coast Mariners were one of the first to take notice of the Kuol brothers.

The Mariners signed the eldest, Alou, first, back in 2019, and then sold him to VfB Stuttgart in 2021. The same year, they also signed Garang before selling him on to Newcastle. The pair's middle brother, Teng, also played for the Mariners and was snapped up by the club in 2021.

NPL clubs like GV Suns focus on player development and moving players on to A-League sides, particularly in the region. Before, if a player didn't have the means to travel or wasn't spotted by an A-League club, they could have easily been missed. But now they have the opportunity to continue their development at a high level and have more eyes cast on them in the process.

Arthur Diles, who worked at various A-League clubs and within academy systems in Australia, knew that the country still faced many challenges to overcome if it was to build on the success of Kuol and co.

One of the biggest challenges is the issue of finances, explained Diles: 'The difficult thing is with some of the migrants from African and similar backgrounds is if they haven't had the financial stability or support to be able to afford to play football because it's not that cheap either to play football in this country, some of them could get lost.

'And maybe there's a lot more talent out there than we're aware of, but we haven't been able to see because they're not right in front of our eyes playing in like the NPL competitions or in competitions that you know everyone's aware of when they look at the talent.'

Another issue is the lack of professional coaches and scouts working in the game.

Diles continued, 'I think as well we're understaffed and we don't have the luxury to have scout to go out and look for these players and scouts for them all over the country so you know that's difficult, too.'

Given Australia's gargantuan size, the country still hasn't been able to recruit enough manpower to cover every region. Even with the introduction of the NPL, Diles still believed a lot of talent was being lost due to a lack of accessibility and a lack of eyes on the sport as well, 'It is crucial I think to get exposure and make sure talent doesn't go to waste. In the UK if Premier League clubs miss out on a player, then you got the Championship clubs. They've got an opportunity to find them. If they miss out and then there's a League One club, then there's a League Two club. Then there's a National League club. If they all missed a talent, it's quite rare that someone would be at that high level, because there's so much, so many clubs and so many eyes that are looking at players. Here in Australia, there are 12 A-League clubs, who are scouting players.

'Only a few of them have scouts. There'll be one or two that have full-time scouts employed and the rest don't even have that. And if you don't have contacts and ears on the ground to know what's happening, you're definitely missing some players here and there.'

But while there has been a lot of challenges, the likes of Kuol, Irankunda and Toure, who have come through the system in spite of the odds, have been a shining beacon of hope. There have been high hopes thrust on their shoulders. All it takes is one or two players to make a mark at the biggest clubs, and the level of interest and scouting from abroad will increase.

With more eyes on talent in the country, there will be more suitors for prospective Australian talent, and in turn more money flooding into the game through an increase in transfer sales. All of that, of course, is easier said than done.

'Australia is a country for me, in my opinion that should be a selling country, and the [A-League] a selling league. It should be a country that just looks to develop and produce and sell,' Diles agreed.

Australia has been moving in that direction. During the 2023/24 A-League season, the record for the most expensive transfer sale of all time was broken twice. Marco Tilio signed for Celtic for €1.75m, and then later Nestory Irankunda made his move to Bayern Munich for €3.4m. With Jordan Bos moving to KVC Westerlo for €1.3m in the same season, becoming the fifth-highest transfer from the A-League of all time, there were definitely signs that Australia was moving closer to Diles's vision.

Another sign is the emergence of an exciting new generation of coaches inside the country. Since the late 2010s, a plethora of Australian professionals have gone abroad to try their luck.

Diles said, 'We've been known for the last 20 to 30 years as a "little" football country in the world that has produced many players to Europe but never really produced any coaches. And you know, in the last five years, you can count on the number of Aussies that went abroad and did well on one hand probably.

'But I think we're just at the beginning of, you know, something special happening within Australian coaches as well.'

One of the poster boys of this new age has been Ange Postecoglou. A dual Australian and Greek citizen, he had grown up in Melbourne after his family fled Greece in 1970 due to a military coup.

Like many immigrants, Postecoglou took to football and played for South Melbourne, for close to a decade. At one point in time he was even managed by the late, great Ferenc Puskás. Upon retirement from playing, Postecoglou went straight into management. He took charge of South Melbourne before working in Australia's youth setup with the under-17 and under-20 sides.

Later, Postecoglou would go on to manage in the A-League at Brisbane Roar and Melbourne Victory before being appointed as the senior national team manager of Australia. Despite helping the country qualify for the 2018 World Cup, Postecoglou announced his resignation from the post in 2017.

A month later he accepted a role working in Japan's J.League with Yokohama F. Marinos. Postecoglou enjoyed a terrific three years in charge and attracted attention for his innovative approach and style. So impressive were his performances that in June 2021 Celtic decided to appoint him as their head coach. Initially, his appointment came under scrutiny, but Postecoglou quickly won the fans over, winning the Scottish Premiership in his first season and then in his second as well. All in all, in two seasons at Celtic, Postecoglou won five trophies, and just two years after his appointment he left for pastures new to join Tottenham Hotspur in the Premier League.

Taking charge of Spurs, Postecoglou became the first Australian to manage a Premier League club.

'We've now infiltrated the Premier League,' Diles said. 'The reaction has been massive. Hopefully, it makes other club owners and fans in Europe and Asia recognise the value of Australian coaches and look at them with a different eye.'

Since Postecoglou's success, the likes of Kevin Muscat and Michael Valkanis have also gone abroad to work in Europe. The latter was even appointed as assistant manager of Ajax. Meanwhile, Muscat briefly worked as manager of Sint-Truidense in Belgium, before moving on to working in the J.League with Yokohama F. Marinos. Others have also started to make names for themselves abroad, not just in the men's but the women's game as well.

While Australia hasn't quite got to where it aspires to be, there is a positive trend towards football evolving in the country. The emergence of young stars like Garang Kuol, the performances at the 2022 World Cup and coaches like Ange Postecoglou proving themselves in Europe have all been examples of that.

As the game grows, there will be more Kuols, Irankundas, Toures and Postecoglous coming through, and a new golden generation should only be around the corner.

# 14

# Morocco

CRISTIANO RONALDO walked off the pitch with his head pointing at the emerald green turf beneath him. His eyes were narrow and his lips pursed. Things had not transpired the way the Portuguese icon had envisaged

The 2022 World Cup in Qatar was supposed to be Ronaldo's last hurrah. His last chance to lift the trophy everyone covets above all. But in the end, Ronaldo's last dance came to an abrupt goodbye in the quarter-finals.

Heading into the game against Morocco, Ronaldo's side were by far the more fancied to progress. Morocco had done well to get to this stage after beating Spain in the last 16. But no African team had ever made it past the quarter-finals. This was when giants like Portugal and Ronaldo took centre stage.

Morocco knew they were the underdogs. They had been the underdogs in almost every game they had played at the World Cup so far. But that had not stopped them against Belgium, Spain nor Croatia. They had come with a plan to frustrate Portugal and did exactly that for 90 minutes, forming a blockade in front of their own goal and bursting into quick counterattacks to catch their opponents on the break.

In the end, all Morocco needed was one chance. Towards the end of the first half, Yahia Attiyat Allah delivered a high looping cross into the Portuguese box. The Portuguese goalkeeper, Diogo Costa, came out to gather, but Youssef En-Nesyri leapt above him and headed the ball into the back of the net.

Morocco celebrated, and went into the break with the advantage. It was an advantage they held on to in the second half, fighting for their lives as Portugal became more and more agitated. Even Ronaldo, who was introduced in the 51st minute, couldn't find a way through.

As he walked off the pitch after the final whistle, the tens of thousands of Moroccan fans packed inside the Al Thumama Stadium were going delirious. Their team hadn't just thwarted one of football's biggest pantomime villains, they had made history. Morocco became the first African team to win a World Cup quarter-final and advance to the semi-finals.

To many, Morocco's moment in the spotlight may have come as something out of the blue. Even perhaps a fortuitous achievement based on mere luck. But in reality, the country had been building up to this moment since 2007.

Back then, Morocco's football fortunes were completely different; they had not qualified for a World Cup since 1998. Meanwhile, in the Africa Cup of Nations, they had failed to go past the group stage in four out of the last five tournaments between 2000 and 2008.

It was clear something had to change. Morocco has always been a proud footballing country. It is home to widely supported clubs like Raja Casablanca and Wydad Casablanca and has a rich history dating back to the early 1970s on the international stage. During the 1970 World Cup, Morocco became just the second African country to qualify for the tournament after Egypt participated in the 1934 edition. They did not taste much success at that World Cup, finishing bottom of a group with West

Germany, Peru and Bulgaria. However, that experience would prove to be a catalyst for Morocco, later winning the first, and so far only, Africa Cup of Nations in the country's history, in 1976.

Two decades later, from 1997 until 1999, Morocco were also the highest-ranked African team according to the FIFA lists, even breaking into the top ten when qualifying for the World Cup in 1998.

Historically, among African countries up until the 2022 World Cup, Morocco had appeared in the second-most (six) tournaments behind Cameroon's eight.

However, by 2007, those achievements seemed like the remnant of a bygone era. So, along came the king of Morocco, his majesty Mohammed VI, an avid follower of the sport. Together with the Moroccan Football Association, Mohammed VI wanted to herald a new age for Moroccan football and he did so by establishing his very own academy located in Salé, just on the outskirts of the country's capital city, Rabat.

Construction on the state-of-the-art project took around two years to complete, and the academy started to welcome talents in 2009. In the process, its staff, led by Nasser Larguet, went on a prolonged scouting mission all across the country to spot the best up-and-coming young talents. Among the first generation were the likes of Youssef En-Nesyri, Azzedine Ounahi and Nayef Aguerd – players who would later shine at that historic World Cup in Qatar. The former even scored that iconic goal against Portugal in the quarter-finals.

From the moment it was established the Mohammed VI academy had always functioned as a live-in college. Prospective players would live in-house and would not only train regularly but also receive important education and schoolwork.

Spaniard Xavi Bernal worked in Morocco for close to seven years. He first started out at the academy in 2014, before working himself up to be the sporting director and the academy manager in 2021.

He has seen Morocco evolve as a football nation during his time in the country.

'When I arrived, it was common to play on dirt or synthetic fields in poor condition. Nowadays, Morocco is evolving a lot, having first-class facilities,' Bernal explained.

One of the keys to the academy's success has been the facilities and the environment Larguet and many others helped to establish. Inside the headquarters, Mohammed VI had set up several teams at every age group from under-13 to first-team level.

Before those ages, Larguet set up satellite academies across the country, where the best talents honed their skills from age nine to 12, until they were ready to move into the academy on a full-time basis.

'The academy has great facilities,' Bernal said. 'Mohammed VI can host about 100 players every year and there are enough coaches and educators who can focus in great attention on each individual in every way possible, whether that be school, medical, sports and personal needs.

'There is a great intensity in the daily work of the youngsters; they live as professionals as soon as they come to the academy from the age of 12.'

Young players typically spend six to seven years developing at the academy. During that time the focus is not just on football but education as well. Bernal explained that all players leave with diplomas to ensure that they are just as well prepared for a life outside of football as they are for a life in the sport.

In many ways the academy's setup very much rivalled that of Premier League or elite academies in world football.

There has been a dedicated full-time medical department constantly at the service of the players. Mental health has also been considered with psychologists provided for the players to support them in their development.

In terms of the structure of the teams, there are five age groups in total: the under-13s, under-15s, under-17s, under-19s and under-21s – who are considered the first team. Like at many elite academies, the staff at Mohammed VI have regularly recognised the top talents and play them in higher age groups if they are to have been judged to have outgrown the group which they would otherwise belong to. This ensures there is no stagnation in development: every player is constantly challenged and pushed to their limit to maximise their potential.

Apart from the intensity of the work inside the academy, administrative staff have also been employed to regularly work on arranging overseas tournaments and getting the players to participate in as many European competitions as possible in order to expose them to different styles and levels of football.

Bernal said, 'I think the most important part is consistency in work. They almost always train two sessions a day and bring the player closer to European football on constant tours that take place abroad. The academy regularly travels to Spain and France to play tournaments. There is also a great tournament that is played every year in Rabat inviting the best European clubs. This means that when a player comes out of the academy, they have already had a lot of experiences with European football that makes it easier for them to adapt to it.'

One of the key pillars that has supported the structure of the academy has been constantly hiring the best minds and people in football development. From the early years, Larguet has been a staunch advocate of building a strong coaching and scouting department. His belief has relied on recruiting the best coaches and educators in order to develop the best players possible.

'The great advantage of the academy is that it has a good control of the country in terms of recruiting the best players. It has a large network distributed throughout the country scouting and searching for the best players,' Larguet said.

Working closely with the federation, from the beginning the Mohammed VI academy has not only concentrated its efforts inside Morocco, but outside of it as well. Morocco has a large overseas diaspora and one of the largest migrant populations in Europe with an estimate of around five million Moroccans living abroad.

When Larguet took over at the Mohammed VI academy he recognised the need to not only produce the best players at home, but to attract the best players possible from abroad as well and bring them into the Moroccan youth setup at an early age.

Under him, Madrid-born Achraf Hakimi was convinced to switch his allegiance to Morocco, Dronten-born Hakim Ziyech also switched from the Netherlands to the country of his parents. Both have become the global face of modern-day Moroccan football, representing some of the biggest clubs in the world throughout their careers, from Real Madrid, Borussia Dortmund and Paris Saint-Germain to Ajax and Chelsea.

Given Morocco's large diaspora, many of the players in the country's World Cup squad were born outside of the country. In fact, out of the 26-man group, only 12 were born in Morocco. Out of that group, two grew up and spent the majority of their childhoods outside of Morocco after their families emigrated to Europe. Meanwhile, from the ten remaining players, five were born in or after 1996, making them old enough to participate in the Mohammed

VI's academy's first phase. Of the five players born after 1996, four came through the ranks of the academy: Ahmed Reda Tagnaouti, Youssef En-Nesyri, Azzedine Ounahi and Nayef Aguerd.

En-Nesyri ended the tournament as the top scorer for Morocco, Ounahi started every game except for one, and Aguerd would have probably done the same if he hadn't suffered an unfortunate injury in the last 16, having proved a formidable presence at the back up until that point.

'In the Moroccan national team there are few players who have developed their careers in Morocco, but the vast majority of players in the national team who have trained in Morocco are from the academy. That is a significant fact to show the importance and quality of the work at the academy,' Bernal explained.

The 2022 World Cup was undoubtedly the crowning achievement of Mohammed VI's academy to date. But given that it had only been functioning properly for just a little bit over a decade up until that point, there has been hope that Morocco's success at the tournament was just the beginning for a new golden generation.

A year later, Morocco won the under-23 AFCON, qualifying for the Olympics in 2024. The same year, the country's under-17 side reached the final of AFCON, qualifying for the World Cup with nine players in the squad coming from the Mohammed VI academy. Later, at the under-17 World Cup, Morocco reached the quarter-final stage, narrowly being defeated by yet another nation covered in this book – Mali.

Those younger generations have undoubtedly been inspired by the performances of the senior national team in Qatar. With Mohammed VI's incredible work over the last decade, interest in the sport has grown. The academy has provided a tangible pathway for young players to escape poverty and created opportunities that hadn't existed before.

'Winning or losing is more important since football is experienced as a means to survive and help the family, not just as a game,' Bernal said.

With strong foundations the Mohammed VI academy has inspired others in Morocco to revamp their football development, too. Some of the country's greatest teams have since placed more emphasis on developing young talent and giving them opportunities at senior level, while there has also been increased scouting across the region to spot new talent.

'Nowadays, Morocco is evolving a lot,' Bernal said. 'More and more the big clubs are beginning to be more concerned about grassroots football and more academies are being created.'

That can only be a positive for the future of Moroccan football, and there is hope the 2022 World Cup was just the first chapter in what may become a glorious saga in the country's footballing history for decades to come.

*From Dinamo Zagreb to the World Cup Final: Mario Mandžukić and Luka Modrić celebrate beating England at the 2018 World Cup.*

*Mitoma's acrobatic assist for Japan's winner against Spain at the 2022 World Cup*

*Alphonso Davies celebrates scoring Canada's first ever goal at the FIFA Men's World Cup back in 2022.*

*Han Kwang Song playing for Juventus' reserve team in a Serie C match back in 2019.*

*The Gambian players celebrate after reaching the knockout rounds of the 2021 AFCON.*

*Khvicha Kvaratskhelia celebrates with his team-mates after Georgia qualified to UEFA Euro 2024 by beating Greece.*

*Azzedine Ounahi celebrates reaching the semi-final of the 2022 World Cup with Morocco after beating Portugal.*

*Dominik Szoboszlai and Marco Rossi celebrate after Hungary secured qualification to Euro 2024 against Montenegro.*

*Uzbekistan's young stars celebrate knocking England out of the 2023 U17 World Cup.*

*Raphael Lea'i representing the Solomon Islands at the 2019 U17 World Cup in Brazil.*

*Thomas Rongen with his American Samoa team during the filming of* Next Goal Wins.

*Mohamed Salah celebrates qualifying for the 2018 World Cup with Egypt.*

# 15

# The New Age

ILIMAN NDIAYE picked the ball up, beat one man, then another, and another, and another. He ran through them like they were practice cones, until there were none left and there was only one thing left to do – tee up his team-mate to score.

To those who had watched him do this hundreds of times on the beaches in Senegal, to the parks in Marseille and the cages of London, this was nothing unusual. Runs like that from Ndiaye were as normal as breathing oxygen. However, to the millions tuning in to watch Senegal at the World Cup against Qatar, this was a new name who had just announced himself on the world's biggest stage.

There were 831 players (Iran were the only team not to use the full 26-man squad, taking just 25 players) who went to the 2022 World Cup – a record high at the time. But none had as tumultuous and as fairy tale of a journey to get to Qatar as Ndiaye.

Four years before appearing at the World Cup, Ndiaye didn't even belong on the books of a professional club. Instead, he was playing for a YouTube team at grassroots level, Rising Ballers FC, which had been founded in that very year.

The club didn't even begin as a club. Rising Ballers was initially started by brothers Brendon and Eni Shabani, along with Jamie Pollitt, as a social media page. The Shabanis had started a page on Instagram with the intention to raise awareness of and appeal to followers of academy football.

Pollitt joined the project after his rival blog, Football Prospects, was spotted by Brendon and Eni and they convinced him to join forces. Very quickly, the project reached mass appeal, with the trio working not just on Instagram but multiple social media platforms, including YouTube and TikTok, and the brand skyrocketed to popularity.

With its focus driven towards rising young prospects, the group also wanted to build on their success and begin an initiative to do even more. In 2019, they founded their own football team from scratch.

The intention with Rising Ballers FC was to help the players who had been released from academy football, and give them another chance to put themselves in the spotlight.

With tens of thousands of subscribers, the team quickly garnered interest. Over 5,000 applications were sent in to play for the club, which was whittled down to the best 20 players. Among them was Ndiaye, who at the time was on the periphery of non-league side Boreham Wood, but was aspiring for more.

'He was the talk of the town,' Mahrez Bettache, Rising Ballers' head coach, remembered.

'He played five-a-side with Gim [another player in the squad] somewhere around Fulham or Hammersmith and apparently everyone was talking about him there. Gim brought him down for Rising Ballers and the rest is history.'

When Bettache saw Ndiaye in action he immediately recognised a lot of potential in the attacking midfielder.

Bettache said, 'I was awed by his fluidity, how dynamic he was and how comfortable he was with both feet. You can tell a footballer by the way he runs. He just fit the profile.

He was very silky with the ball. Probably the best freestyler-slash-footballer that I know to this day. The things he does with the ball are just incredible.'

But what appealed to Bettache even more was Ndiaye's behaviour on the pitch. He may have been flamboyant in his style when playing football, but off the pitch Bettache saw a muted, down-to-earth character, who was determined to make it in the game.

'He was very shy, very humble. Even now he keeps himself to himself and he just lets his feet do the talking,' Bettache explained.

But while Bettache was immediately convinced, the feeling wasn't mutual. Ndiaye wasn't initially sold by the Rising Ballers project. He wanted to break into professional football and what Rising Ballers were attempting to do at the time was unprecedented. Bettache, though, was eager to change his mind, 'He wasn't sure the club was for him. But then I remember the first time I met him I had a conversation with him. I spoke to him about what my vision was and what I wanted from him. I told him I wanted him to be our star man, who we really focused on. Not just on the pitch but off it too in terms of the media side of things. In the end, he came on board and before we knew it, he left us as well.'

Rising Ballers' offer of a platform to put players like Ndiaye in the eyes of an audience who was already invested in the development of young players, and were aficionados of the genre, was an appealing one.

In an ever-increasingly social media-dominated world, Rising Ballers' access to millions of followers across multiple platforms gave the opportunity to these players for a second chance to attract the attention of scouts.

The club uploaded weekly episodes on YouTube of their progress as they went to play academy and grassroots clubs across the country. Immediately, the team captivated viewers with their individual talent and skill on show. An impeccable first touch by one of Ndiaye's team-mates, Darius Johnson, while playing in a game for Rising Ballers went viral and was viewed by over 500 million people across various social media platforms. As a result, Johnson earned a trial at Chelsea, and then later ended up signing for Eredivisie club FC Volendam, where he fought to become a regular in the side. Later, Johnson even became a fully fledged international, representing Grenada. Not bad for a player who prior to joining Rising Ballers had only played at Sunday league level.

Ndiaye's story was similar. Born in France to a Senegalese father, he first represented Marseille at academy level at the age of ten. But then the family decided to uproot back to Senegal.

Ndiaye spent his formative teenage years playing on the beaches of Senegal, before his family decided to move again. At 14 years old, Ndiaye and his family arrived in England, which initially proved to be a culture shock for the teenager. At the time he spoke little English, and it took him time to adjust to a different life, let alone a different way of playing the game he loved. In those years, Ndiaye's talent was very much overlooked. In the end, he was signed through Boreham Wood's PASE college programme, and there he caught the attention of his coaches as someone with the potential to have a bright future in the game.

During one match held at St George's Park, designed for Premier League referees to get to grips with the VAR system that was set to be introduced, Ndiaye stole the show. His dazzling run, beating multiple players before finishing the ball into the back of the net, was what Bettache would soon become accustomed to seeing at Rising Ballers, and what Ndiaye would later do at the World Cup.

'I had big aspirations for him,' Bettache said. 'I must admit, he was very talented, but he was very raw at the time – he needed coaching. No one could get him off the ball, but we really had to hone down on his actual game, and what he could deliver, which we then saw later on at Sheffield United and Senegal.'

At Rising Ballers, Bettache worked extensively with the club's young players to get them in the best shape possible, not just for the showcase games for the club but also for potential trials at professional teams.

Bettache said, 'We also did lots of one-to-one sessions working on his finishing and explosiveness and those kinds of things. And we worked on basic stuff like in-game information as well. I would send him videos or clips of players that I would like to imitate in his game. Players like [Zinedine] Zidane, cultured and creative players who can make a difference. Sometimes at the beginning he made it very hard for himself. In the beginning he had to take on two or three players to get that shot off, whereas nowadays he is getting his shots off without having to do too much of that kind of work. So, it was just down to showing him how to utilise the skills that he has because at the time he was doing too much unnecessary work.'

Ndiaye was quick to pick up Bettache's advice. Together they spent the summer of 2019 on the training ground, with Bettache helping Ndiaye get in the best shape possible. On the pitch, that was reflected with some excellent performances which made Ndiaye one of the standout players for Rising Ballers.

Through the club's network, Rising Ballers was able to secure trials for Ndiaye at various clubs including Sheffield United, then of the Premier League. The Blades saw enough in Ndiaye to offer him a contract and bring him to the under-21 side.

There Ndiaye worked his way through the ranks, establishing himself as one of the club's best players at under-21 level and slowly but surely earning opportunities for himself at first-team level as well.

There were hurdles along the way, but throughout it all Bettache and Rising Ballers stayed in touch and helped to support him through the challenges.

Bettache said, 'His journey has been very quick. I didn't think it would be that soon. There was a period at Sheffield United when it was 50-50 on whether he would get a new contract. We were having light conversations on WhatsApp, and we told him he needed to crack on. And he listened to that advice, doing extra gym work, doing extra work on the pitch after training rather than going home for lunch.

'And then very quickly I remember the Snapchats he was sending me in his first camp, and he was just in awe being around Sadio Mané and everyone else. But he also knows he belongs there, and he deserves his place.'

In a short amount of time, Ndiaye went from playing for Rising Ballers on parks and 3G pitches around London to making his debut in the Premier League at the King Power Stadium against Leicester City. Then he later helped Sheffield United get promoted from the Championship and played at the World Cup.

'The journey through a college programme and a grassroots team to the World Cup, I don't think many players can do that. We are now talking about maybe the one per cent, he is part of that, where he can comfortably say he is a footballer. Many players fall at various hurdles but he's really grasped his opportunities and made them count,' Bettache said.

Many would argue these were opportunities that without the support system and exposure from Rising Ballers, Ndiaye would never have been able to get.

The initiative has since grown in success, and over the years it's not just Darius Johnson or Ndiaye who have benefitted from Rising Ballers' platform. Tom Chiabi ended up signing for Sunderland after representing Rising Ballers. Youssef Chentouf signed for Wigan Athletic and Jayden Clarke joined Gillingham, even scoring for them in the FA Cup.

'In terms of Rising Ballers and the platform they have, that's always been their goal – to bring in players like Iliman with bundles of talent, who for some reason have slipped through the net, and work together to try and help get them a professional contract,' Bettache explained.

'It's a family. A small, tight-knit group. Even to this day we keep in touch with one another.'

Over the years dozens of players have gone on to sign professional contracts after representing Rising Ballers. Meanwhile, the club have grown in status, becoming a semi-professional team and working their way up the non-league pyramid – all thanks to the power of the internet.

Rising Ballers is, of course, not the first club to build a fanbase and support through the internet. Spencer Owen's Hashtag United have enjoyed a similar rise, but Rising Ballers are the first who are building a team based on the promotion of young talent, and the first to have given the platform for players to sign professional contracts at Premier League clubs.

Their work must be commended. They have created new avenues and pathways for young players, and have helped players like Iliman Ndiaye achieve dreams they may never have thought possible.

But it's not just on YouTube that players are gaining more exposure. The power of social media has meant that even without a platform like Rising Ballers, players can put themselves in the shop window and in front of the eyes of relevant people much easier than before.

Take Scott Chickelday's story as an example.

A few years ago, Chickelday was enjoying a regular weekday afternoon. He casually scrolled through his Instagram-browsing social media as one normally does, not looking at anything in particular – the usual posts and captions blotted his screen full of a myriad of memories and frozen moments in time. Then all of a sudden a message popped up from a 15-year-old boy in Norway named Jens, asking, 'What do you think of my clips?'

Chickelday, who worked as a coach and had stints at clubs like Tottenham, has received dozens of messages on his Instagram of players trying to get his attention on a regular basis. But he was captivated by this one. The message was accompanied by a video depicting a showreel of a blond-haired kid with flair and talent. Scott saw potential and he was immediately interested to find out more.

'I was like, wow this kid's unreal, and I said to him, "Why have you sent me this?"' Chickelday recalled.

The boy was brunt and straight to the point, 'I want to come to England. Can you get me a club?'

Chickelday was a bit reticent, asking, 'Well, maybe I need to speak to your dad first?'

The kid replied, 'I want to prove myself, bring me to England.'

But Chickelday was insistent. 'Ultimately I spoke to his dad,' he said. 'And he was like, "Oh, I'm sorry, Jens is so determined." In the end I talked to a few clubs, and I managed to arrange him a trial.'

The boy in question was Jens Petter Hauge, who would later end up signing for AC Milan and play in the Serie A before moving to the Bundesliga with Eintracht Frankfurt.

But back then he was on his way from the perpetually cloudy Norway and his hometown of Bodø to travel thousands of miles across Europe to Berkshire.

'I got him a trial through my friend at Reading Football Club,' Chickelday explained.

'He came over and he went into their academy, and he tore it to pieces. I remember I watched two games, and he was absolutely phenomenal.'

Naturally, coaches at Reading's academy were thoroughly impressed by how this kid from Norway, who came out of nowhere, was able to settle in so quickly and dazzle everyone with his skills.

This being prior to Brexit, Reading were keen to bring Hauge in and sign him immediately. According to sources, they offered Hauge a contract. However, his parent club at the time, Bodø/Glimt, wanted €10,000 as compensation and Reading were reluctant to agree at that price range. In the end, the club offered to include the compensation fee in the contract in instalments, but Bodø continued to haggle and demanded it to be paid upfront.

Ultimately, the two clubs came to a stalemate and Hauge went back to Norway without a deal.

'When he went back Jens told me, "I'm going to stay in Norway. I'm going to get in the first team, and someone will buy me from England." That's how much Jens believed in himself,' Chickelday recalled with a smile.

Hauge's prediction would prove to be right, though. He used the trial and the disappointment of the deal falling through at Reading as motivation to work his way up to Bodø/Glimt's first team. He made over 100 appearances before Italian giants AC Milan decided to snap him up.

'I think he came to England, saw the level and went back to Norway determined to come back,' Chickelday said.

On and off the pitch the experience at Reading was undoubtedly a crucial one for Hauge, and one that would never have come about years prior without the influence of social media. His story is again an example of how the internet and social media has shaped the modern game.

Ultimately, Ndiaye and Hauge have been underdogs in their journeys to the top, and their ability to rise up the ranks has undoubtedly been benefitted by the power of the internet.

Social media provides an endless array of networking opportunities and millions of eyes on potential new talented footballers, which,, built on top of the myriad of scouting databases like Wyscout and InStat that cover hundreds of leagues all around the world and provide statistical data on hundreds of thousands of players, gives more exposure to players around the globe than ever before.

Stories like Hauge's at Reading have become almost the norm. Agents and scouts often first interact with prospective players on social media, or spot them by watching and analysing their data on scouting platforms.

Meanwhile, social media accounts like Rising Ballers help provide exposure to talents and put them in the spotlight.

Undoubtedly, there are still many issues our contemporary world has to contend with regarding the increased influence of social media on our everyday life, but in this realm social media has provided youngsters with endless possibilities and opportunities to catch the attention of the right people. It has even helped one of them reach the World Cup and another secure trials in England. The stories of Iliman Ndiaye and Jens Petter Hauge are the stories of the future, and the beginning of a new era in the game.

# 16

# The Republic of Ireland

ON THE turf of the Nándor Hidegkuti Stadion, the Republic of Ireland's players slumped to the ground as the referee blew the final whistle. They had given it their all, stretched every sinew of their muscles, but were awarded with nothing.

Spain had run them ragged and thrashed them 3-0, which had meant they were eliminated from the 2023 under-17 European Championship.

Despite the disappointing result and the elimination, the Republic will look back on the tournament with pride. The country's young stars impressed and went all the way to the quarter-finals, beating the likes of Wales and Hungary en route.

In the end it was the influence of Lamine Yamal and Marc Guiu that would make the difference between the two sides. Both scored in that game and would then go on to break into Barcelona's first team the following season, scoring important goals for the Catalans.

For the Republic of Ireland the tournament would also prove to be a significant turning point. While this was not the first time they had reached this stage of the competition, back in 2019 they played in the group stage of the under-17 European Championship, and a year prior they even made the quarter-finals.

However, what was different about the 2023 Republic of Ireland team compared to the 2019 one was its make-up. In 2019, just two players in the squad represented clubs in the country, with the majority plying their trade in England. In 2018, it was very much the same. But in 2023 that number skyrocketed; a total of 18 players represented clubs in the Republic of Ireland, with only two playing abroad.

The rapid shift can be attributed to many things, but it mainly had two origin stories.

The Republic of Ireland's radical shift started in 2015. In that year, after months of dithering, Jack Grealish made a decision that changed the outcome of his career. Having come through the Republic of Ireland's national youth setup, the Aston Villa academy graduate decided to accept the call of the Three Lions instead – in what was the ultimate betrayal.

Grealish's decision to turn his back on the Republic of Ireland was only made more sour by Declan Rice, who similarly had represented the country even at first-team level, following in his path a few years later.

'There's no ill will from our point of view towards those two,' Will Clark from the Football Association of Ireland and League of Ireland explained. 'But from a strategic point of view it did make us realise we could not always rely on our diaspora.'

Albeit perceived treacherous moves, neither Grealish nor Rice could reasonably be argued against for making the choice that they did. The Republic of Ireland has been a country with a great footballing history. The national team even made the quarter-finals of the World Cup in 1990, while players like Roy Keane, Robbie Keane and Niall Quinn have all been produced.

However, by the time Rice and Grealish were forced into a decision the Republic of Ireland had fallen into the shadow of its past.

From the turn of the century until 2024, they had won just two games at major tournaments. One came at the 2002 World Cup against Saudi Arabia, and the more famous one was against Italy at the 2016 European Championship.

Other than that, Irish fans have had little to cheer about. The first two decades of Irish football in the 21st century can be categorised as simply one disappointment after another, from Thierry Henry's infamous handball for France during the qualification process for the 2010 World Cup to an embarrassing 5-1 defeat to Denmark in the plays-offs for the 2018 World Cup and finishing level on points with Luxembourg during the 2022 World Cup qualification process, a whopping eight places off Portugal in second place.

Looking at it from that perspective, the Republic of Ireland doesn't necessarily come across as a country on the rise, nor as an underdog ready to surprise everyone on the big stage.

But in the aftermath of those rejections by Grealish and Rice, its footballing landscape has changed radically, and there are hopes the country's struggles will soon be in the past.

One of the key factors that has impacted Irish football was the United Kingdom's decision to leave the European Union – which was voted on in 2016 but only came into effect in 2020.

Brexit not only changed the political landscape in Europe, but it very much transformed the Republic of Ireland's footballing strategy. Up until Brexit, English clubs have had a hegemony on the best Irish talent. For much of the 20th and 21st centuries, the top players developing in the Republic of Ireland at grassroots clubs were quickly snapped up and brought to English academies for relatively low transfer or compensation fees.

But in the aftermath of Brexit that hegemony had eroded. Prior to Brexit regulations coming into effect, before 2020 British teams were able to lure a young Irish player once they had turned 16 years old as per EU rules. However, post-Brexit, that's no longer possible. Now English clubs are only able to sign Irish players when they have celebrated their 18th birthday in line with FIFA rules, thus completely losing their monopoly in the market – especially against other EU clubs.

'So pretty much in Ireland we've always had a really strong tradition of grassroots football and international football and but typically what would have happened in the past, like decades, kids would have played for some really, really good grassroots clubs and then the best players at like 15 or 16 would have obviously gone primarily to England,' Clark said.

'The likes of Robbie Keane, Richard Dunne and Shay Given – all those lads would have gone to England at 16 and that's only actually recently changed because of Brexit because the UK are no longer in the EU and the FIFA regulations don't permit the transfers of minors outside of the EU. But before that, during the last 50 or 60 years, the best Irish talent would have gone to England at a very young age.'

England's pilfering of Irish talent, while beneficial to the best young players who were able to join top clubs at a young age, was detrimental to the development of professional leagues in the Republic of Ireland. With the best players leaving to go abroad, there was little incentive for professional clubs to develop talent they were likely to lose before they even got close to the first team anyway.

As a result, the League of Ireland, which is the Republic of Ireland's professional league, saw its growth stunted and left decades behind, something Clark was determined to change when he was appointed as a development manager within the FAI.

'The league has actually been quite niche and there was never really any sort of focus in terms of youth developments,' Clark explained. 'The clubs here, pretty much they were basically like a men's first team and they would have maybe reserve teams, but there were no academies, there was no youth development. That would have been perceived to be the responsibility of the grassroots clubs. So, we've never really had that sort of tradition I suppose in the professional part of the game.'

Brexit changed the consciousness of the way people viewed the league and the way professional clubs have approached their own player development. Within the FAI it was also an opportunity to start anew.

Fuelled by the rejections of Grealish and Rice, the FAI wanted to create a sustainable model inside the country – which would not rely on the acquisition of Irish diaspora players.

Clark said, 'If you look at a lot of Irish kids who went away over the years, you know they would have had massive potential. But for a host of reasons, they could not fulfil their potential. I think largely it was because of a lack of support. They were living in a different country, and they found they had to settle into things very quickly. Whereas now, obviously post-Brexit players can't go to England until they are over 18 years old.

'So, when the players do go over, they're obviously here for longer. And now there's more emphasis on it being a more holistic approach. We're really strong on players completing their secondary-level education and giving them a firm footing if you like, from an educational point of view. Whereas in the past, kids going to England at 16 they would have had to sacrifice a large part of their education to be honest with you and it didn't work out, because they put so many of their eggs in one basket.

'So now I think our players will be going over [to England] a little bit more mature, a little bit more prepared for what it's like living in another country.'

While kids have received important education, they have also been exposed to senior football at a much earlier age post-Brexit in the Republic of Ireland. Previously, a 16-year-old Irish player would have only had experience at an academy or grassroots football club prior to moving abroad.

However, post-Brexit, with the FAI's developmental changes in the League of Ireland, the country's young stars have been snapped up by the best professional clubs at home and, in return, they have also been given opportunities to play senior football at a much younger age.

Brighton's Evan Ferguson made his debut in senior football in a friendly for Bohemians against Chelsea at just 14 years old. He then became the youngest player to debut in the League of Ireland at 14 years and 11 months old. Since Ferguson, a further three 15-year-olds have made their professional debut in the top flight of the League of Ireland in Jaden Umeh, Mason Melia and Sam Curtis. The quartet have become the youngest players to ever make an appearance in the League of Ireland – with the previous record belonging to Gerry Hill, who was 16 years and three days old when at the time of his first appearance back in 2002.

'A lot of the top young players, they're getting a lot of first-team football in the League of Ireland. For example, Andy Moran, who went to Brighton, he would have played senior football for Bray Wanderers at 15 years of age for the first time,' said Clark.

That experience at first-team level has become an important learning curve in the development of the Republic of Ireland's new generation of players post-Brexit.

Clark continued, 'It's definitely an advantage to Irish players. The fact that they are getting first-team football opportunities at a much younger age. So, when the kids go and they maybe play in England or they're playing in France or Italy rather, that little bit of first-team experience and playing in front of crowds, sort of being around professional players, definitely helps them settle in and definitely makes them a little bit more prepared than they would have been in the past.'

But while there have been many advantages of Brexit, it has also thrown up a lot of new challenges in Irish football. Since the changes have occurred so fast, the Republic of Ireland has very much started this new model from scratch – which means the country started decades behind the top countries in world football, and closing that gap has needed time, patience and investment.

Clark said, 'One of the negatives that we have is that the academy system at the minute is still very much in its infancy. We've got big issues in relation to the physical infrastructure within the country. You know, the facilities are not what they need to be.

'To be fair to the FAI, they are really ambitious and there are plans in place to change that. But we're seeking state help at the moment in terms of trying to improve the infrastructure in the country – and that's because some of the facilities at the moment are really worse than substandard, to be honest.'

Having state-of-the-art pitches can aid the development of players and encourage more kids to pick up the sport.

Away from the facilities the Republic of Ireland has also struggled with a lack of human resources.

'Most of the coaches coaching in the academy system are working part-time, even the ones that are qualified. We also have minimum requirements in place. So, for example, if you want to coach at under-19 level, you have to have an A licence. It's also an A licence for under-17 and it's a B licence for under-14 and 15,' Clark said.

'A lot of these coaches would be part-time volunteers. We only have nine full-time and youth development coaches working in the country. So, we're basically trying to develop the best players we can, with little infrastructure and with limited coaching contact time, and we're relying on the best endeavours of volunteer coaches to give the players the best development experience they can.'

A lack of high-quality coaches available has meant young kids have not always been given the same footballing education as their peers elsewhere across the world.

Clark added, 'The fact that the players are still very much only coming in part-time is a problem as well. The kids are not getting as much coaching contact and that has an impact on their development.

'Up until maybe sort of 15 or 16 years of age, it's still nowhere near where it needs to be compared to other countries. A typical Irish kid, he might get maybe three nights' coaching in a week. Probably, maybe six hours' coaching contact a week, which again would be miles behind their counterparts around Europe at that particular age.'

The fact that in spite of this the Republic of Ireland has been able to continue to produce high-quality players and compete in tournaments like the under-17 European Championship is demonstrative of the brewing raw talent inside the country. It has also highlighted the potential to grow and become even greater in the coming years.

With players like Evan Ferguson, who has made waves in the Premier League, and other Irish youngsters following suit, the Republic of Ireland can build a new golden generation once again.

Clark said, 'I do think things will change in the coming years. There's never been a doubt about the quality and the potential of our players. We've always had really good players and we are a football nation. Football is the number one sport in the country and even from a coaching point of view, we've got some really, really good coaches who've done an unbelievable job developing the players of the quality that we have in almost a voluntary capacity.'

Importantly, the Republic of Ireland's future has now finally returned to its own hands. Whereas beforehand there may have been an over-reliance on England, and the country's diaspora across the seas, in the future the goal is to make Irish football more sustainable and to create an environment where the country can cultivate its own stars.

'For the first time we are actually in charge of our own destiny, and we never had that before,' Clark concluded.

What remains is a blank page with endless possibilities.

# 17

# Egypt

MOHAMED SALAH took a deep breath, licked his lips and looked up at the goalkeeper in front of him. The 86,000 fans packed inside the Borg El Arab Stadium waited in anticipation. That number was only a small fraction of the 109 million people who were watching from afar glued to their television screens around Egypt.

The country's fate rested on Salah's shoulders. His team were just an inch away from qualifying for the World Cup for the first time in almost three decades. All the Liverpool legend needed to do was put the ball in the back of the net from 12 yards.

The match between Congo and Egypt in 2017 was full of drama. For an hour the two sides fought each other tooth and nail but to no avail, before the Pharaohs struck, with Salah finding the back of the net. Egypt defended with their lives in the remaining minutes. Congo, though, never surrendered. They kept plucking away and in the 87th minute they equalised, wrenching a cruel dagger in the hearts of millions of Egyptian football fans.

There would, however, be one last twist. Egypt were awarded a penalty three minutes into added time when the Congolese goalkeeper hacked down Trézéguet inside the penalty area. Up stepped Salah with the weight of expectation from 109 million people on his shoulders. But he showed nerves of steel and thundered the ball into the back of the net.

The scenes inside the stadium and all across Egypt were rapturous. Football has always been the country's most popular sport dating back to 1934 when Egypt became the first African nation to participate in the World Cup, and that football heritage was retained for much of its history, listing the Africa Cup of Nations a record seven times. But a return to the World Cup, a tournament they had only participated in twice prior, had always been the dream – the wish that most Egyptian fans had yearned for – and Salah had finally made it come true.

Despite only being 25 years old at the time, it was Salah's crowning moment in an Egypt shirt, which cemented his place not just as a football star but as an icon. That's something he would have probably found unfathomable even just a few years prior. Salah's story of how he became the man to take Egypt back to the World Cup is one of a man overcoming the odds time and time again, and never ever giving up.

Salah grew up in a tiny village in Egypt called Nagrig. It had a population of less than 10,000 people – compared to the country's enormous population, that figure is miniscule.

During Salah's childhood, Nagrig was stricken by poverty and very much sheltered from the rest of Egypt. Despite being relatively closely situated to the country's capital, Cairo, the journey to get there was a long and arduous process that took two and a half hours on bus or by a car through rutted dirt tracks.

Salah wasn't born into a poor family. By the village's standards he was middle class and never had to starve. From a young age he had been infatuated by the game and spent hours practising around the village on dirt tracks and narrow alleyways.

At 14 years old he was eventually spotted by a scout from Al Mokawloon, and signed for the club. But during the first few years of his time there he encountered many challenges.

One of those was that gruelling trip from Nagrig to Cairo which Salah had to take every day to get to training and back. With his parents busy at work, Salah had to take four to five buses in total in a return trip that lasted for around five hours.

Yet in spite of the challenges, Salah continued to progress at Al Mokawloon. His talents were always recognised, but it would be under one Frenchman of Yugoslavian descent that his fate would change completely.

When I spoke to Ivica Todorov, he recalled vividly the first time he saw Salah in the flesh as if it was yesterday.

It was a hazy evening in Cairo. Todorov had gone to watch a group of boys playing on a yellowed-out turf on the edge of the city. He'd just arrived in Egypt and was appointed as manager of Al Mokawloon. He was eager to find out about the young talents at his disposal, but not quite used to the sweltering heat of the city. Sweat dappled on Todorov's forehead but the coach was paying no attention to it. His eyes were fixed on a small streak zipping across the boys on the right flank of the pitch, demonstrating the kind of quality he had come to find.

Salah had only come on as a late substitute in the game but he immediately caught Todorov's eyes with the way he bolted across the field over and over again, leaving defenders tumbling to the ground in his wake.

'When I arrived at the club I was missing players,' Todorov recalled. 'So, I went to see a junior match and this boy came on with the game at 0-1. In 16 minutes, he scored a goal and gave an assist. I asked who he was, and they told me, "Mohamed Salah."

'I told him straight away to come directly to the first team and train with us. I could tell he was special.'

By the time Todorov invited Salah to Al Mokawloon's first team the young attacker already had a bit of experience at senior level, but he was still on the periphery of the squad. The club's previous manager, Hamza El Gamal, did not favour the Egyptian youngster and had demoted him to the reserves.

When Todorov met Salah in training next he quickly realised that had been a mistake. Todorov was impressed not just by Salah's quality but the way the teenager slotted in and handled the new environment around him. He was completely dedicated to his profession and set the standard in the training sessions, showing the kind of attitude that Todorov was looking for, 'He came to training the next day and arrived an hour earlier than anyone else. I was impressed.'

During Todorov's time at the club, Salah's early appearances in training and games would become a regular occurrence. But he was not in a rush to leave the training ground either.

Todorov said, 'After games and training, he would often stay in my locker room, and he would ask questions about what he can still improve. It motivated him, he was eager to learn. Sometimes, he would stay behind after training to work on his control and hit balls all by himself.'

Despite the long hours spent at the training ground, Salah was never exhausted. He had been used to the gruelling regime of travelling back and forth from a young age. By the time he was training with Todorov, the club had found him a place of abode in Cairo, which gave Salah even more time to spend in practice.

'He never complained,' Todorov explained. 'He always wanted to work more.'

It took Todorov just five days to be convinced by what he saw of the Egyptian. He started Salah in the club's next game against Al Ahly, and the youngster did not let him down.

After a looping long pass, Salah ran in behind the opposition's defence and controlled the ball with immaculate precision.

'He scored to make it 1-1, I remember he ran over to me and thanked me just as everyone was congratulating him,' Todorov said.

Todorov's influence would prove to be the catalyst for Salah's breakthrough at senior level. He gave the forward the trust and confidence he needed to shine.

From early on Todorov also recognised that Salah had the potential to go far in the game, and he embraced the young man and encouraged him to play to his strengths.

Todorov said, 'In football, there are a lot of players who can go fast with the ball at their feet. Mohamed can go very fast, but where he is different from the others is that he can also change direction at an exceptional speed.'

According to Todorov this was innate in Salah, 'The speed was the only thing that we did not work on, it was natural for him. He had this unique ability and you could tell it was a special gift.

'I am sure that he was born with something that the others do not have. He never stopped working throughout his career and you can see he was eventually rewarded for his hard work.'

Aside from the innate ability, it was Salah's attitude which stood out to Todorov above everything else. Salah simply wanted to work more than the rest. He wasn't just infatuated with football like most players – he was obsessed. But still he still needed an arm around the shoulder from someone who put their faith in him and allowed him to spread his wings.

'After sessions I would always take the opportunity to talk to him and he wanted to listen. I think those talks gave him the confidence to do the things he was doing in training in match situations as well,' said Todorov.

'Sometimes younger players develop an ego when they are given a chance in the first team, but he never had that. After he started playing, he just wanted to play more and more and he did not care about anything else.'

This is something Todorov insisted had always remained with Salah, even after he had become one of the most recognisable faces in the game, 'In many ways he has changed now. He is one of Egypt's best players, but even today I can tell he has remained very humble.'

Thanks to Todorov's belief, Salah would quickly grow and progress in Egypt during what was a fraught time for football and politics inside the country. At the same time as Salah was making his progress the political landscape in Egypt was changing.

In 2011 a revolution was sparked which led to the resignation of Egypt's dictatorial leader Hosni Mubarak, and the beginning of a new democratic era. During the interim period the country underwent military rule and there were mass protests and violence in football stadiums across Egypt.

This culminated in the Port Said Stadium riot which saw Al Masry and Al Ahly fans storm and clash on the pitch and resulted in the deaths of 74 people, with 500 injured. The tragedy led to the suspension of the Egyptian Premier League which meant Salah and his team were unable to play.

By then Salah was one of the biggest emerging stars in Egypt. He had attracted the attention of several European sides, and Basel in Switzerland used the suspension as an opportunity to take a closer look at him, arranging a friendly against the Egyptian Olympic team. Salah only played in the second half but scored twice and helped Egypt win 4-3. Those 45 minutes were enough to convince Basel, who signed Salah a month later after a successful trial period.

At Basel, Salah would go on to even greater heights and two years later he would make the step up to the Premier League, joining Chelsea and becoming only the seventh Egyptian to sign for a club in England's top flight.

But Salah didn't immediately reach the heights he would go on to achieve later on in his career. At Chelsea his game time was limited with manager José Mourinho never really favouring him. Instead, Salah would be sent out on loan to Fiorentina and AS Roma, and he was later sold to the latter. Roma then sold Salah to Chelsea's rivals Liverpool a year later, where he eventually found his home at Anfield.

The rest is history. Liverpool gave Salah the tools to establish himself as one of the greatest players of the 21st century and to become an icon in Egypt. During the late 2010s and early 2020s few players had been able to rival Salah's attacking output and individual and collective honours.

When I spoke to him, Todorov regarded his protégé as one of the best players in the world, 'He has been working with one of the best coaches in the world. I think he is among the best players in the world, and I hope he wins the Ballon d'Or one day because he is a golden boy.'

Salah's journey from Nagrig to being recognised among the world's elite players has been the stuff of Hollywood movies. For Egypt, he hasn't quite been able to lead his country to the kinds of accolades he would have wanted. But his moment against Congo gave millions of people living in Egypt the kind of joy they hadn't experienced in decades, something that they will remember for the rest of their lives. Ultimately, that is what football has always been about.

In the end, Egypt's return to the World Cup in 2018 may not have amounted to much. Salah's side crashed out of the group stage after losing all three games. But Salah himself produced commendable performances scoring two goals in three appearances – which made him the joint top scorer for Egypt in World Cup finals matches alongside Abdelrahman Fawzy, who scored twice at the inaugural World Cup in 1934. It also meant he had contributed to one third of Egypt's goals in the history of the tournament overall.

The fact that a boy from a small village has been able to achieve all of that through so many obstacles to represent a nation of over 100 million people is without a shadow of a doubt one of the greatest modern underdog stories in the football world.

And there are many chapters still left to be written.

18

# Solomon Islands

SURROUNDED BY turquoise water, beaches with white sands and spectacular coral reefs, the Solomon Islands has always been a paradise, the kind of place where affluent tourists have flocked to.

Made up of a group of archipelagos located in the South Pacific, since the turn of the century the Solomon Islands has also been a country in a constant state of survival. With rising sea water levels, the nation has had to battle the elements as hazardous cyclones and floods wreaked havoc on its population, while many of its citizens live without access to clean water or electricity in their homes. Every year, the high tides have affected more and more inhabitants and have left more homes at the risk of flooding, which has meant more and more people have been faced with the choice of either staying on the islands under difficult circumstances or fleeing – even if there has been nowhere else to go.

Juliano Antonio Schmeling worked for Marist FC, a local club on the island. Before that, he was the country's national futsal coach. He explained: 'Solomon is a small country geographically. Most people live in the capital Honiara – that's where most of the opportunities are. Some of the other smaller islands are very small communities. Most of the islands are not very developed at all even in Honiara some areas are still very disadvantaged.'

In those conditions, and the harsh impacts of climate change, football has offered an escape from the harsh realities of the living conditions on the island – but also a more tangible physical escape from the island itself by earning a move overseas.

'Football is a passion for the country,' Schmeling said. 'They live and breathe football here. It's their favourite sport – the most popular one by far. They also see it as an opportunity to get out of the country. Many players move on to neighbouring countries to pursue careers in Australia or New Zealand. Normally, kids grow up dreaming of getting contracts and earning money by moving to those countries.'

But while most players have dreamed of making it to Australia and New Zealand, during Schmeling's time on the island there was someone who had even loftier ambitions.

Schmeling first met Raphael Lea'i when Raphael was just a little boy, playing on the fields of the islands.

'Some of my players told me I needed to watch this kid. He was playing some community games at the time, so I went to his match, and I was really impressed. Immediately, I invited him to train with us,' Schmeling said.

Lea'i was a unique talent who had honed his skills playing futsal and street football. The former is actually a more popular and accessible sport in the Solomon Islands, and it's where the country has enjoyed a lot more success, qualifying to four consecutive World Cups between 2008 and 2021. But Schmeling recognised that Lea'i had an ability not just to play futsal but football as well. The teenager just needed someone to support him in the endeavour.

Schmeling said, 'He came to training, and he was really good. From then on, I started to build a relationship with him. I also started to investigate his life because he came from a different island. He was living in Honiara with his uncle and some relatives, but he didn't have the proper conditions.'

After his investigations Schmeling saw that Lea'i needed more than just an arm around his shoulders. He had been living under difficult conditions which often made it difficult for Lea'i to pursue his dream.

'He was living in a house with no heating, or water in the village. So, I went to my wife and spoke to her and told her, "Look, there's a nice boy here, with a big talent and we need to help him," and she agreed with me, and we invited him to live with us,' Schmeling explained.

No longer dealing with the disadvantages of having to travel long distances to training and often not even having the means to get there, living at Schmeling's house meant Lea'i could concentrate on football and train every day.

Schmeling said, 'Technically, you could see the talent straight away, he had good individual skills, and he was fast as well. But what really got my attention was his attitude. I met so many people on the islands who always gave me some excuse because the reality is that the country is really difficult to get around and they joke here about "island time" because most people end up never arriving on time due to the traffic or not having money to go to the bus.'

Lea'i, though, never had this attitude. Even at a young age he was determined to play his beloved sport and take advantage of his opportunity.

Schmeling continued, 'From the beginning when I invited him to train with us, he would do anything to be there on time. I remember the first time I told him to be at my place at 5pm to have a chat, and he was there on time sweating. He arrived all wet and I asked him how he came and he told me he ran all the way just to get here. So that was like a different attitude. Because he didn't have the money or anyone to drop him off but he still made sure he got there on time through whatever means he could.

'That moment made me realise he was a different kind of player, a different kind of attitude. After that I saw every day that he was a completely different person [compared to other players] and I could tell that he was going to go far because of that. His attitude and his fighting spirit – that's what made me believe he could make it. Because technically I have seen many other equally talented players here on this island, but no one with the same drive as him.'

Initially, when Schmeling first met Lea'i, the young boy had played a lot of futsal, but he didn't have a lot of experience playing actual organised 11-a-side football. During his first few weeks under Schmeling, Lea'i would undergo an intensive course to understand the principles of a more complex form of the game.

At the time, Schmeling had invited a few former Brazilian professional players to play on the island at Marist FC, and it was through them that Lea'i was gradually introduced to full-time training and learning the basic principles and physical requirements of football.

'It was a good way to introduce Raphael to that kind of environment,' Schmeling explained. 'He learned a lot from them just about what is needed to become a professional footballer.'

Only 14 years old at the time, Lea'i flourished under Schmeling's guidance. Quickly, he broke into the first-team environment and at just 15 years old he scored four goals in his first six senior league games for Marist.

He then went on to score 26 goals in ten games the following season for Henderson Eels at just 16 years old and in the same year finished as the top scorer of the under-16 OFC Championships, scoring eight goals in five games and being named the Best Player of the Competition.

In the process Lea'i also made history. The Solomon Islands finished second in the tournament which meant they qualified for the under-17 World Cup. This was the first time the Solomon Islands had ever qualified for a World Cup at any level in the sport.

The Solomon Islands' under-17 team may have lost every subsequent game at the World Cup in 2019, but Lea'i still did enough to impress scouts. His constant energy was a threat to opponents, and he showed he was capable of holding his ground against the best players of his generation at the highest level of the game as well.

Lea'i went back to the Solomon Islands after the tournament and scored 33 goals in 20 games during the 2020/21 season. If it wasn't for the Covid-19 pandemic restricting travel he may have moved abroad then, but he ended up staying on the islands for two more years, scoring 12 goals in seven games the following season and then 22 goals in ten.

By that point Lea'i was only 19 years old but he was already a fully fledged senior international who had scored four goals in four games in World Cup qualifying. It was at this point that Lea'i would go on to achieve what none of his fellow countrymen had done before him.

In January 2023, Lea'i was finally snapped up by a club from abroad. He signed for the historic Velež Mostar in Bosnia – a club that during the 1970s and '80s had been recognised as one of the best in the Yugoslav league and had also marched as far as the quarter-final of the UEFA Cup.

Lea'i's signing was a groundbreaking moment in the history of football on the Solomon Islands, becoming the first player from the nation to earn a professional contract in Europe.

Instantly, he became a sensation not just back in his homeland but in Bosnia as well. Lea'i scored a goal and registered an assist on his first start for Mostar, which saw the club's supporters chanting his name in the stands.

He also caught the eye with his silky touches and ability to beat his opponents one vs one. In total Lea'i only spent six months at Mostar, and while his performances on the pitch were a resounding success with a goal contribution every 77 minutes on average, off the pitch he struggled to adjust to his new environment and climate.

The experience will have been a learning curve for the young man, and it's something Schmeling believes Lea'i will have used as inspiration as he embarked on the next chapter in his career, 'He is in a very crucial moment, and I hope he can keep going.'

The incentive is there for Lea'i to accomplish even more in the game. But already, at such a young age, he has also become an inspiration for others in his homeland.

Schmeling said, 'His example is the kind of example Solomon needs. The people here love him, everyone recognises him and respects him. They need these kinds of inspiration more. He is a good example, and a perfect role model for the younger generation. On and off the field, he is a very good person. He doesn't drink, he doesn't smoke – he is someone who looks after himself very well who likes to push himself and is very disciplined.'

There is a long path ahead of Lea'i and the Solomon Islands, but the achievements of the previous few years from appearing on the world stage at the under-17 World Cup and signing that contract in Europe are all pointing towards the right direction.

Historically, the country is still very much a toddler in comparison to the football nations of the rest of the world. The national team had only been founded in 1978. It became recognised as part of FIFA a decade later, and from that moment onwards football has always been a popular sport. But given the islands' geographical situation, the evolution of the game has been slow. The country's first semi-professional league was only established in 2000; it has historically consisted of 12 teams, mainly located in the capital city, Honiara, with eight in total from that region.

Since its foundations in FIFA, on the international stage the Solomon Islands has always been a minnow. The country's highest recorded ranking was 120th place. But there has always been ambition to grow the game further. The 2010s have definitely seen huge strides made in that regard, which have given the tools to players like Lea'i to make it as far as he did.

The results have also started to improve. During the 2022 and the 2018 World Cup qualifying campaigns, the Solomon Islands came second behind New Zealand and missed out on a spot from the inter-federation play-offs by a small (although often big based on the scorelines) margins.

In future years, the Solomon Islands may have an opportunity to go a step further. With FIFA expanding the World Cup to 48 teams from the 2026 tournament, Oceania has been granted one automatic spot for the first-placed team in qualification. Meanwhile, the second-placed team has an opportunity to enter the inter-federation play-offs and fight for a place at the finals.

Schmeling said, 'I think in different parts of the world they didn't accept or like the news [about the expansion] much. But here in Oceania and the Pacific region everyone loved it. Obviously, we understand that right now New Zealand is above the rest. But for countries like Solomon this is still a game changer – because it's never been done in history and it's an opportunity in so many different ways to play at a higher level, to earn the attention of scouts, and to test themselves.'

The prospect of countries like the Solomon Islands getting to those play-offs, and putting themselves in with a chance of making it to football's ultimate stage, adds more fuel and inspiration for players who previously may never have dreamed that such a prospect was even possible.

But everyone inside the country understands that there is still a long way to go if such dreams are to be fulfilled.

'You have the top clubs who have some kind of development and finances, but even they still struggle a lot with the facilities. Some of them have their own fields, but most of them share the facilities with schools or some community fields. Only the top two or three clubs have their own facilities,' said Schmeling.

The country has benefitted from more investment by FIFA since the 2010s, as well as overseas benefactors including China. The latter's funding saw the building of a new national stadium, replacing the Lawson Tama Stadium – famous for the fact that its stands were built into the side of a hill. The national stadium was built for the 2023 Pacific Games and opened in that year. It is a state-of-the-art modern construction – it comes with stands which can host up to 10,000 seated spectators, and it was a gift to the Solomon Islands from China.

'It's a beautiful stadium,' Schmeling said. 'It's quite a miracle for the Solomon Islands to have a stadium like that. So now that's where all the national team games are held, and the league matches as well.

'The last few years, the development has changed a lot. FIFA has now introduced more programmes and brings in more coaches to teach the kids. People are trying to improve the conditions here.'

While investment and funding has helped, Schmeling still believes there was a long way to go until the kids on the islands can fully flourish – not just on the pitch but off it as well, 'They have schools on the island, but the reality is that a lot of kids come from very small communities. They don't really have proper experiences in school. They play on the field all day long and they develop their own skills by themselves. Very few of them get the education they deserve.

'But I believe there is a lot of raw talent here, and a lot of potential.'

A place at the World Cup still seems like a long distance away, but the Solomon Islands definitely made a step in the right direction. Having already competed at the World Cup at youth level, there is a flicker of hope that one day Raphael Lea'i and his generation can write history on the senior stage as well. Schmeling certainly believed they had a chance, 'The experience from under-17 level can definitely help. If Raphael's generation can do that now at senior level, it would be a miracle, but it's not impossible.'

# 19

# Luxembourg

SOME PLAYERS were on their knees looking up at the heavens. Others were embracing each other with beaming smiles. Around them, jeers and whistles reverberated inside the Bilino Polje Stadium.

Nobody had expected Luxembourg to travel to Bosnia and win during the Euro 2024 qualification process. Just a few months earlier they had suffered a 6-0 defeat at the hands of Portugal. Bosnia were the home side and the favourites. A few months prior, when they had last played at home, they had defeated Iceland 3-0 during their first game of the qualifying campaign. They were regarded as one of the favourites to qualify out of the group stage. But now the stadium was echoing in boos.

That's because on 17 June 2023, Luxembourg didn't just snatch a victory: they dominated Bosnia and deserved to win by more than the 2-0 scoreline in their favour.

Luxembourg's manager, Luc Holtz, had played for his country for years before taking over as the head coach of the national team. In his playing days, a result like this would have been inconceivable. But on that day, this wasn't the pinnacle of Luxembourg's qualifying campaign. It was just the start of a historic process in which Luxembourg came inches away from reaching a major tournament for the first time.

'It was the beginning of something. Bosnia was the big favourite. And we went there and won 2-0. After that everybody started to feel that we can make something special,' Holtz recalled.

Nestled in between Belgium, France and Germany, Luxembourg has been one of the smallest countries in Europe since its foundations with a population of just over 600,000. In football, the national team had always been considered as a minnow. Even by securing that victory over Bosnia, Holtz and his side had already achieved something that Luxembourg had never achieved in the 21st century – winning more than one game in European Championship qualifying.

But this wasn't a mere fluke. Luxembourg had been on a steady rise for several years prior and the 2024 qualifying campaign was just yet more proof of the tremendous growth that the country has achieved since the beginning of the 2010s.

The person who has seen this first-hand from the very beginning has been Holtz himself. Born in Luxembourg, Holtz represented the national team in over 50 games for almost a decade. When he was appointed as manager in 2010, he had already worked for two years as head coach of Luxembourg's under-21 side. But initially, he had his work cut out for him.

In 2010, Holtz inherited a team that was largely amateur or semi-professional. It was a team that couldn't even fathom the idea of even getting one or two victories in the qualifying process, let alone being in with a chance of getting to a major tournament.

'We're a small country. I think a lot of people, they think we have to stay always small. We are a little afraid of doing things we are not used to do,' Holtz explained.

'Even when I played in the national team, we were always a little afraid. We have always been afraid because we think of ourselves as small and so we thought other teams, they must be better than us and we didn't take any risk of doing things to even try to win.

'I think this is the culture of the people in the country. The first step is always to be secure of what you are doing. Even our kids at school. They always prefer the secure choice rather than taking a risk.'

During Holtz's time as a player, he had become accustomed to Luxembourg's attitude of approaching games with the aim of not losing or losing by 'only' a few goals. Very rarely did they set out to win.

He said, 'When I played for the national team, we always played defensive football. Our objective was to defend, to defend and to defend. Don't take any risk because we will lose. You'll get too many goals and that was always the mentality.'

When Holtz took over as manager of his country, he was desperate to change that mindset, 'So, my vision was to start changing things. I think the biggest step to change things was to give more confidence to our players, to play higher up the pitch and to play more offensive football.'

Holtz didn't inherit an easy job. When he was appointed, Luxembourg were ranked 117th in the FIFA list and were the seventh-worst team in Europe. The country's national team was made up of players plying their trade either in Luxembourg or in the lower divisions of German, Belgian and French football, mostly on a semi-professional basis.

Instantly, Holtz recognised that if Luxembourg were to improve, then a new strategy had to be adopted. He didn't just have to instil newfound belief, he needed to change the entire make-up of football in the country. Luxembourg simply needed more players playing at a higher level.

In order to achieve this, the Luxembourg Football Federation organised a football school from under-13 to under-19 level. The best players in the country were selected to attend programmes every week from Monday to Thursday. The players were not only given high-level coaching, but regularly played fixtures against the best academies of nearby clubs from Germany, Belgium and France.

The innovative method saw the best youngsters often only playing for their club sides during the weekends, and spending most of their development years within the tight-knit community of the Luxembourg Football Federation.

'We have a football skill school here in Luxembourg. During the week our youth team, they play against foreign teams. A lot of time against the German teams or against French teams, against Belgian teams, sometimes a little bit further like Dutch teams or sometimes even against Italian teams,' Holtz explained.

This programme has paid dividends for Luxembourg. Not only did it create absolute cohesion between age groups and allowed for an easier integration into the senior national setup, but it also provided more eyes on the club's brightest stars and gave them the exposure to prove themselves against the best academies from neighbouring countries.

'Because of this we get more young players out of the country to join professional clubs in foreign countries. That's one reason why we can improve.'

Subsequently, talented players have earned moves to top academies in Germany, Belgium and France – and thus benefitted from even more high-level coaching and more competitive environments where they could develop and enhance their talent.

'It was a long process,' Holtz said. 'Thirteen years ago, we had only one professional player [in the national team]. At the time, one of my targets was to get more players out of the country, to have more professional players in higher leagues because it's only that way that we can develop something and improve ourselves both individually and collectively. We took it step by step and we got more and more professional players.'

By the Euro 2024 qualification process, Holtz didn't just have a team of professional players to call up, he also had several who were playing at the highest levels. Leandro Barreiro and Mathias Olesen are two examples. They were both playing in the Bundesliga at the time for Mainz and FC Köln respectively. Meanwhile, Gerson Rodrigues, who became the first Luxembourg international to appear in the group stage of the Champions League, was also part of the squad.

But they are just a few names among many players who were competing in top European divisions or elite academies in European football. Considering that a decade prior Luxembourg just had one professional player in the national team, this was a rapid acceleration of the country's footballing fortunes. Holtz believes changing demographics have been a key factor in the development.

'The migration of people in Luxembourg has been a big factor,' Holtz said. 'We have a lot of people from Portugal and from Cape Verde, who came to Luxembourg, and then there is also ex-Yugoslavian immigrants like Bosnia and Montenegro. We have a lot of players from those nations here in our youth department and the first team.'

Luxembourg's changing demographics have definitely created more diversity in the national team. Roughly 60 per cent of the players who make up Luxembourg's squad were either born outside of Luxembourg or are first-generation immigrants.

All of these changes have helped Holtz build a team with a new face and a new identity. More importantly, the team is not plagued by the mental burdens of the past, and is full of young players writing a new chapter in the country's history.

During the Euro 2024 qualification groups, Luxembourg's average age was just 24.2 years – this was the youngest out of any team competing. One of those players, Yvandro Borges Sanches, was also among the five youngest players to score during qualifying.

Holtz embraced Luxembourg's burgeoning young talents and gave them an environment where they were able to experience elite international football at a very young age, to learn on the job and grow from their mistakes.

'I don't look at the age of a player. I look at quality. When you have a guy who is 17 but I think he has the qualities to make a good career and that he can help our team, I will take the player even when he is 17,' Holtz said.

'I know a young player who is 17, 18 or 19 years old – he will do mistakes because he is not as mature, or he has not had that experience like 32-old-players. But it's part of development. I think for a player who is 17 or 18 years old, and who has high quality, the best thing is to play. He needs to play, he needs to make mistakes, but he needs to learn from his mistakes and it's the fastest way to develop, to become a professional player.'

The new generation led by Holtz have given Luxembourg's supporters a new lease of life. A decade ago, the average attendance for national team games was less than 1,000 – sometimes merely a few hundred people turned up. But now, Luxembourg average record attendances and regularly sell out the country's state-of-the-art national stadium – the Stade de Luxembourg – which can host close to 10,000 people.

'It [the support] has been completely crazy,' Holtz said. 'What has happened in Luxembourg is actually crazy because when I played in the national team, we had about 2,000 people when we played in a game. The only exception was when we played one of the big countries like Portugal, then the stadium was full. But now this year [2023] we had five times the stadium was full.'

This newfound love for the game has undoubtedly helped his team's success on the pitch as well. The extra support galvanised Luxembourg to greater heights during the Euro 2024 qualifiers. Fans played a key role in helping the team secure important victories at home to Bosnia and Iceland, which were crucial in helping them finish above the two nations – who in the previous decade had both qualified for major tournaments including the World Cup.

Holtz said, 'This is something really new in Luxembourg that the fans are following our team and are supporting our team and getting behind them. That's something when you talk about changing the mentality. The mentality is very positive. Like I said before, a lot of times the fans, the media and everyone else had a negative view of our football, and that's completely different this year. I've felt the supporters, so positive, really supporting the team.'

But the supporters haven't just been key in big matches. Even against smaller opposition, they have come out in their droves and had gotten behind the team.

Holtz continued, 'Even in the game against Liechtenstein. We played 70 minutes, and we were still 0-0 in a game the fans were expecting us to win. Before, maybe they would have given up, but in this game the supporters stood by us. They were positive the whole time and that helped us to win the game. In every game they have been very, very positive and we use them as the 12th player on our side.'

Apart from the qualifying campaign, another factor that has helped increase fan participation has been the introduction of the UEFA Nations League, a biennial tiered competition, broken up into four divisions with separate groups – all competing for promotions and qualification to a final.

Luxembourg started out in the bottom division, but earned qualification to the third tier, and they will go into the 2024/25 competition as top seeds in that division after a successful campaign in 2022/23. That alone shows the level of progress Holtz's side have made over the years.

But there are more benefits to the Nations League. One of them is that it pits teams of equal parity against each other in competitive matches. This gives players experience and an understanding of how to perform in high-level and pressure situations.

On top of that, for countries like Luxembourg the competition has offered that tiny vestige of success – and something to celebrate and galvanise the nation. Previously, competitive football for nations like Luxembourg consisted of finishing in and around the bottom of qualification groups for major tournaments. But now there is a competition where Luxembourg can vie and compete for the top spots.

Holtz said, 'I think playing against teams with a similar level helped us improve because we won a lot of games, so naturally you improve. It helped us especially with the confidence. Also, because it's a game on a high level, but not too high for your team so you can move and grow step by step. So, my opinion, especially for our country, we have played now three times in the Nations League, and all three times it was very interesting and very useful for us. Because we were always able to grow and were also very close to moving on to the B league.

'And every game was very, very exciting and decisive to get the first place. We are still in Division C, but I think the target for the future for the Nations League will be to make the first place to go up to Division B. But that's also a very new situation for us, because we have never been in a place where people expected us to get first place. So, it's going to be interesting.'

As well as creating more competitive games and helping to bridge the gap in European football between the smaller and bigger nations, the Nations League has offered an alternative route to qualifying for a major tournament for countries like Luxembourg. The highest-ranked teams in the competition have a chance to qualify for the European Championship through the play-offs.

So, while despite a historic qualifying campaign Holtz's side failed to qualify for the 2024 European Championship through the group stage, finishing five points behind second-placed Slovakia in third place, due to their high ranking in the Nations League they earned a spot in the play-offs.

For the first time in the country's history, in 2024 Luxembourg played a play-off match with the chance of competing at the European Championship.

'It would be complete crazy,' Holtz said before the game, 'if Luxembourg made it to the European Championship. I think the whole country would be crazy and supporting the team because it never happened and it would be something really, really new and special.'

Luxembourg's opponents in the play-off semi-final were Georgia. Playing away from home, Holtz's side were up against the odds, as they had been many times before. Unfortunately, in the end it proved a step too much, with Georgia running away 2-0 winners. But for Luxembourg this was just the beginning of their journey. They will continue to aim for qualifying for the European Championship, and as the country grows their chances will continue to increase.

Holtz concluded, 'I think a lot of people are very impressed by what a small country like Luxembourg can do. But now the next step is to qualify for a European Championship. That would be something really great, because all those people who still think that we are a small country, maybe if we managed to do it, even those people may actually start to change their minds. And slowly, the mindset will start to change even more.'

If Luxembourg continue to grow at the same rate as they have grown since the 2010s under Holtz's leadership, they will have every chance of fulfilling that dream. And the country's qualifying process during Euro 2024 will have been just the beginning of a new chapter and a new era in Luxembourg's football history.

# 20

# Saudi Arabia

WITH HIS back to goal, Salem Al-Dawsari twisted around one Argentinian defender. As he pirouetted inside the penalty area, he skipped past another, the ball sticking to his feet like an extension of his foot.

The crowd were already up on their feet. Those who knew Al-Dawsari knew what was going to happen next. Every sinew of muscle in his thighs and calves stretched taut – like the strings of a bow. There was nothing Emiliano Martínez could do. The moment the ball left Al-Dawsari's foot it was only heading one way – thundering into the back of the net – to herald an eruption of cheers inside the Lusail Stadium.

Saudi Arabia's victory over Argentina in the opening game of Group C at the 2022 World Cup sent shockwaves around the world. It was greeted with jubilation back home. Tens of thousands of fans celebrated around the ground in Qatar as well.

The Saudis had achieved plenty of surprise results at the World Cup in the past. Saudi Arabia's footballing history is abundant with success. But this was special. This was quite possibly the heralding of a new era, where Saudi Arabia can come up against the best in the world and still conquer.

The man tasked with heralding that new era is Romeo Jozak. The Croatian's achievements speak for themselves. As addressed in this book, Jozak transformed Dinamo Zagreb's academy, turning it into one of the best in world football. His subsequent programme developed in the national team saw Croatia achieve unprecedented success at the World Cup both in 2018 and 2022.

But after leaving his homeland, Jozak sought a new challenge, and in Saudi Arabia he found the ambition and drive that he craved. In 2021, he became the talent coordinator of the country's football federation, where he has played a key role in Saudi Arabia's ambitious project. As part of his role, he also became the technical director of the Future Falcons programme, a Saudi Arabian Football Federation initiative that recruits the top talents from the country and places a special emphasis on helping them develop and receive the best possible education to be able to compete at youth international competitions.

'The project itself is amazing. It's truly amazing,' Jozak told me in early 2024. 'I've been in football as you know all my life and I've really been doing everything. From all that I've seen from top to bottom, I can say that the programme itself is something that is simply extraordinary.'

Jozak has visited every top club on the planet and wrote a footballing curriculum that is widely taught and studied all over the globe. When it comes to player development there are few people as knowledgeable as he is in the world of football.

But he has stressed that he has never been a one-man show. Jozak has always had the ability to recruit staff around him who are capable of executing his vision. At Dinamo Zagreb, he would spend months scouting potential coaches. In Saudi Arabia, he has brought in trusty advisors as well to work alongside him.

'My involvement, I wouldn't want to call it my involvement only,' Jozak said. 'Because there's a lot of staff around me. I'm a technical director, that's true. But the people that are working with me, they're really top-level people with real dedication and focus and we really want to take the country from B to A.'

Alongside Jozak, the Saudi Arabian Football Federation (SAFF) also hired the equally renowned Nasser Larguet, who worked for many years establishing and building Morocco's golden generation that went on to reach the semi-finals of the World Cup in Qatar.

Together with Jozak, the two of them have made a star-studded cast, but they're just the main players in an extremely well-organised structure full of members who are at the top of their professions in the sport.

The high-level appointments are another marker of Saudi Arabia's footballing ambitions. Since the late 2010s, Saudi Arabia has made a constructive effort to develop the nation's game.

Football has always been the most popular sport in Saudi Arabia. The country is also home to some of the most widely followed and popular teams in the region, including Al Hilal and Al-Ittihad. But as Jozak said, Saudi Arabia has aspired to go beyond its successes of the past. To reach from B to A.

One of the most seismic shifts in the Saudi Arabian game happened in the aftermath of the 2022 World Cup. Shortly after the tournament, on 30 December 2022, Al Nassr announced the acquisition of Cristiano Ronaldo. The Portuguese forward, still very much at the height of his game having scored 18 Premier League goals for Manchester United in the previous season, was regarded as a huge coup for the Saudi Pro League.

Building on the excitement from beating Lionel Messi at the World Cup, Ronaldo's arrival brought even more football fervour to Saudi Arabia. But Ronaldo coming to the league was just the beginning.

Later during the 2023 summer transfer window, Saudi Arabian clubs caused a sensation in the market. That summer, they spent an estimated £760m, which was second only to the Premier League (£1.59bn) and more than any other top-five European league.

This impressive summer of spending saw the likes of Sadio Mané, Neymar, Riyad Mahrez and Roberto Firmino signed up. Saudi clubs didn't just bring in one or two players: the top sides like Al Hilal, Al-Ahli and Al-Ittihad recruited elite stars from Europe's best clubs in almost every position, creating superteams in the process.

Some likened Saudi Arabia's movements to the way China tried to create a footballing monopoly back in the late 2010s. But that was a move which ultimately became merely a fad – and China's ambition waned in the ensuing years.

Jozak believes the same won't happen to the Saudi Pro League, nor Saudi Arabia's ambitions, because of the football culture in the country, and the determination of those in charge to fulfil the ambitious targets that have been set.

'You know China tried a few years ago and they failed. You can't compare China with Saudi Arabia. China never really had a football culture. China had money. But one of my friends, Tom Byer, he always says culture is important, and you cannot buy culture,' Jozak explained.

'Saudi Arabia has talent and Saudi Arabia has culture you've never seen with the fans in China. Yes, of course, when the big team comes but never like they support the country here in Saudi Arabia.

'Here the kids play football on the street, the kids love it. It's by far the number one sport in the country. I'm not sure where football ranks in China, but it's not number one so this is a completely different project, on a completely different scale.

'The people here are very passionate about the sport. Everyone wants to watch the games. In the coffee shops, during dinners, people talk about football. They get together and that's one of the main topics of conversation. The passion is enormous.'

One of the main factors behind the popularity of the sport in Saudi Arabia is that the country is one of the most successful nations in the history of Asian football.

Dating back to the 1980s, Saudi Arabia have won multiple Asian Cups and reached the final a record six times. They have also appeared in a total of seven World Cups dating back to 1994. This is the football heritage Jozak is referring to, the kind of football heritage that is deeply seeped into the ethos and culture of Saudi Arabian life.

'There's a real passion for the game here,' Jozak said. 'They're always going to watch the game. They're playing for glory. It means more to the fans. Even if none of the new stars were here, they would still all go to the game. OK, maybe not as many, but still, the people here are going to follow their clubs and the country no matter what.'

This passion isn't just reflected on the pitch either. It's a passion that is present on the local pitches, and among the thousands of aspiring young footballers hoping to fulfil their dreams.

'Saudi Arabia has over 30 million people and the country has some serious talent, serious passion, mix of everything, tall guys, short guys, fast guys, tough guys. Every mix of talent Saudi Arabia has,' added Jozak.

Since the 1970s and '80s, Saudi Arabian football has always been at the upper echelons within its own continent. The goal for Jozak and his team is to reach the next level, which Jozak was able to accomplish working in Croatian football for well over a decade.

When I spoke to him in 2024, Jozak was only three years into the project. But already he was feeling hopeful about the prospects of what is to come. During his time, Saudi Arabia didn't just beat Argentina at the World Cup – they also won the under-23 Asian Cup in 2022, for the first time.

Meanwhile, Saudi Arabia's young stars have been getting more opportunities than ever before, whether that's through securing trials in Europe or making a mark in the senior league. In the space of a year between 2022 and 2023, the record for the youngest player to debut in the Saudi Pro League was broken twice. In 2022, Jathob Muslet made his debut for Al Batin at the age of 16 years and six days old. Just over a year later Talal Haji broke that record by a day when he made his first appearance for Al-Ittihad. Haji was later included in Saudi Arabia's senior squad for the Asian Cup in 2023, and was the youngest player at the tournament.

This has been an encouraging sign for the direction of football in the country. Saudi Arabia isn't just focusing on bringing in the biggest stars – it's also keen to grow and nurture its own talent.

Another example of this will have been the recruitment at Al-Ahli of one of the brightest young coaches in European football, Matthias Jaissle. Having worked at Red Bull Salzburg and achieved great success with the Austrian club, Jaissle was acquired by Al-Ahli, and has built his team around a mixture of experience and young Saudi Arabian talent with 23-year-old Firas Al-Buraikan becoming one of his key players.

'There's a lot of top-level talent here, very many talented players,' Jozak explained.

In order to best prepare the talent at his disposal, Jozak has very much taken the same pages of his own book and implemented the strategies which had brought success for Dinamo Zagreb and Croatia in the past.

'Everything I did before at Dinamo, it's all here, with the people that I bring including the coaches and the scouts. I am choosing the people who understand and follow our ideas from before,' he said.

On the pitch, Jozak can see the resemblance in quality as well, 'I would say everything is quite similar, maybe not the same. Obviously, not everything will be the same. Because Croatia and Saudi Arabia are two different climates and cultures. However, at the end of the day we are still gathered around the ball – and that's still the core principle.

'The better you handle the ball you're obviously going to be more successful. So the idea right there. Saudis are very talented, very talented nation. They have football in their genes. It's not hard to implement the same football that we played in Croatia. I would say the playing philosophy is very much the same.'

But Jozak understands more than anyone that football is not always played just on the field. So much of success is what happens off it. At Dinamo Zagreb, he would often see talent wasted because they lacked the right attitude or mentality. That's one aspect that he is looking to change in his new role.

He said, 'Football is about the discipline, physical endurance, it's about the structure and it is about the tactics. It's a lot of things other than the ball itself. And that's before we even talk about the mentality. Success is often determined by being mentally strong. That's actually where we're trying to implement and do a lot of work.'

As part of the changes Jozak has made, he has lowered the age group in his Future Falcons programme. Initially, the project started out as an under-19 team, but it has now switched to an under-17 setup.

'The lower you go with the age, the better chance you still have to develop them and change them as players,' Jozak explained. 'Of course, also it's just a realistic fact that when a player is 18 or 19 years old we cannot always get all the best players. At that age players already have contracts in the first team. The best ones are already really highly involved in the local competitions.'

There are other advantages as well, focusing on a younger age group. When Jozak embarked on his new under-17 project, there were ten years left until Saudi Arabia hosted the 2034 World Cup. Jozak's first batch of talent were the 2009 generation, who will be 26 years old by the time the tournament begins – a prime age.

Jozak said, 'We are taking in the 2009 generation first to literally try to aim for the next ten years. They're going to be 26 at the World Cup. Our aim in that time will be to get the best out of them and really start to develop them. Another key objective will be to lower and narrow the gap between Europe and Saudi Arabia.'

The latter is a challenge that Asian football is starting to overcome. At the 2022 World Cup in Qatar, for the first time three Asian teams qualified for the last 16. In the 2026 World Cup, with the numbers increasing to 48, there will be a record number of Asian representatives, and the probability to achieve an even greater result will thus become greater as well.

The rise of Asian football, both at international and domestic level with the introduction of the AFC Asian Champions League, will be key in the development of Saudi Arabia itself and helping the country bridge that gap with European football.

'We are already heading in a really positive direction,' Jozak explained. 'As you know the league is growing and now the second division is growing as well. There are more and more talented young players playing regularly at a really high first-team level. This is a really good sign.'

But Jozak still believes more can be done to help Saudi Arabia reach the next stage in its metamorphosis, particularly when it comes to Saudi Arabian footballers going abroad to Europe in order to prove their mettle there.

He added, 'I always say I'm from Croatia and we have a basketball team. Whenever we had players playing in the NBA, we had a good basketball national team. Whenever we don't even have one player playing in NBA, our national team isn't as good. So the more players participating in the NBA, in a top-level environment, the stronger we are.

'In football that environment right now is Europe. So, I think it would make sense for Saudi Arabia to export young talents to European teams. They don't all have to go to Europe. We can develop really good talent here as well. However, for the players that are really punching above their weight, if you know what I mean, the ones that are playing in Saudi Arabia, the ones that are actually participating in SPL, and not just participating but playing really well, they should go to the level above, and right now that level above is Europe.'

It's a common principle in development. A player grows not when they continue to excel, but when they are constantly challenged and tested. Going abroad and proving yourself in another league away from the comforts of home is one of the best ways to grow, not just as a footballer but as a person.

Jozak made the comparisons to the NBA, but an even more accurate comparison is his own achievements at Dinamo Zagreb. At Dinamo, Jozak and his coaching team gave the tools and the fundamentals to players like Luka Modrić and Mario Mandžukić, which they could then harness as they gradually made the next steps in their career, moving from one top European club to the other and constantly challenging themselves in new environments until they reached the upper echelons of the footballing world.

Of course, in the long term the Saudi Arabian Pro League aspires to become that top level for players in the sport. That development, however, will take time, which is why, in the meantime, increasing Saudi Arabian players playing in Europe could be a great tool for the development of the national team.

But in the long term Jozak believes Saudi Arabia has the means to create an environment where the best players and the best teams are playing in the country, 'The league itself and the academies, they are improving, they're getting better. Facilities are getting better. Everything is going in a really positive direction. This is one of the most impressive projects that I think has ever been made in football. But obviously my job is to look at where we can be even better. Things can always be a little bit better, they can be worse as well of course, but our goal is to always improve. There's always room to grow.'

It's an exciting new chapter in Saudi Arabian football. At the core, though, Jozak has reiterated that the key fundamentals will always be the same. 'The number one thing you need to have is to be able to find the most talented players. Everything starts from that. If you don't have the most talented players, the level you're going to reach is not going to be as big as it would have been. I would say we are already heading in that direction. We already have some really exciting talents in the programme.'

Jozak has set big aspirations for himself. He's got a firm belief that the programme will not only be successful, but leave a lasting legacy in Saudi Arabia for generations to come, 'I want to make a world impact with the programme. Yes, we're already making an impact. You heard about it.

Everybody has heard about it. When I tell people, they're amazed with the programme. But I want to do something not just for me, but to leave a legacy behind for Saudi Arabia.

'I see the enormous potential this programme has. Our advantage is that now we have a lot of time. Most people don't. In football a lot of the times people are thinking short term.

'You need to have something, you know, in a few months or at least a season. But here we have some time to actually do something – we have a long-term goal. We have the talent, we have the resources. We have everything we want and that's why we'd like to make a world impact.

'In our work we can really choose from the best. And when you choose the best from the best you can actually put them in a training process for them to be working and then we can build a real football giant from Saudi Arabia. That's what I'm hoping we're going to become in the future.'

Looking ahead to the 2034 World Cup, Jozak has set clear objectives as well. The goal is the same as it once was in Croatia – to get a medal at the tournament, 'I know the World Cup is going to be huge. We are going to have huge technological miracles in order to make the World Cup a once-in-a-lifetime event. I know it's going to be something never seen before.

'I am hoping we're all going to be alive to be able to see that in person. To be honest, I would be happy if Saudi Arabia reached the semi-final. I will be extremely happy with the semis. I know it's not going to be easy. There are still a lot of things to be done and to be developed. But if overall we do things the right way, prepare everything as we should, I really believe Saudi Arabia has an excellent chance to achieve something special.

'Of course, football can be unpredictable. You can lose to anyone in the space of 90 minutes. However, being in that tournament at home with the eyes of the world watching us over there with everything, with the passion, with the preparation, with involvement, with investments, with everything I would say we should aim for the semi-finals and then winning the third-place medal. To get a medal – that would be an amazing accomplishment.'

Given everything that Jozak has achieved in the game, he has every right to set such immense targets. No one really knows what the future holds, but it wouldn't be a surprise to see Jozak's ambitions turn to reality when the World Cup concludes in 2034. Until then, there is more work ahead.

# 21

# Uzbekistan

UNDER THE Big Arch in Hiroshima, the blue, white and green flags waved high in the air. In the sweltering heat, Uzbekistan's rag team of underdogs embraced each other in smiles. They had done what nobody expected them to do – even their own government.

Back in 1994, as Uzbekistan embarked on the country's first Asian Games, the government was unsure about sponsoring a football team for the event. This was a country still very much in its infancy following the dissolution of the Soviet Union. Finances were finite, and the government wanted to spend it wisely – on teams and individuals who were likely to bring home medals.

The football team, which had not delivered much success in the previous three years since independence, was seen as an unaffordable luxury. In the end, a small pittance of merely £11,000 was spared on the team. The meagre budget meant Uzbekistan travelled to the tournament with the smallest squad possible, consisting of just 17 players, and incredibly just three backroom staff – the head coach, Rustam Akramov, his assistant, Berador Abduraimov, and a club doctor who also acted as the team masseur.

To place the state of Uzbekistan's football team into context, this was also a squad that was very much ravaged by the loss of its top stars. Players like Andrey Pyatnitsky and Valery Kechinov, who was Uzbekistan's golden boot winner in 1992, had switched their allegiance to Russia a year prior. And instead of representing Uzbekistan at the Asian Games they played at the 1994 World Cup in the US wearing Russian colours.

In this environment nobody really expected much of a fledgling country, especially with Uzbekistan coming up against powerhouses at the tournament. Their first game was against a Saudi Arabian side who had made it to the last 16 at the 1994 World Cup earlier that year.

Saudi Arabia were by far the favourites. They had travelled with an under-23 squad, but their team included a few players who had competed at the World Cup and they had high hopes.

Yet Uzbekistan blew Saudi Arabia out of the water; they stunned everyone with an opening 4-1 victory – and that was just the beginning. A 5-0 victory over Thailand followed, and then they backed that up with a 1-0 victory over Hong Kong.

The subsequent 5-4 thriller against Thailand to confirm first place in the group secured what was already a remarkable result. Uzbekistan were the bottom seeds when the draw was made. Nobody had expected them to reach the knockout stages, but Akramov's side had astonished everyone.

Many would have expected Akramov's team of underdogs to sit deep and defend – exploiting counterattacking situations. Instead, though, they took games to their opponents and played exciting attacking football. Using a 4-3-3 formation, Uzbekistan were constantly looking to surge forward and score goals, which made many neutrals take notice.

In the next round they did not need to move mountains to beat Turkmenistan 3-0. Igor Shkvyrin, a veteran 31-year-old forward, scored twice to take his tally to seven goals in five games at the tournament. The victory set up a semi-final where everyone was certain that Uzbekistan's fairy-tale run would come to an end.

Uzbekistan's next opponents were South Korea, who had not spared any expenses to go to the tournament and were the clear favourites. Nine of the players from South Korea's team had also been part of their squad at the 1994 World Cup.

It was a tight affair. Uzbekistan never really turned away from Akramov's principles, playing attacking football and always looking to break South Korea down from the forefront. But South Korea's defence stood resolutely. They had conceded just two goals in the group stage and were regarded as the best back line at the tournament.

In the end, a 65th-minute strike from Azamat Abduraimov, which took a cruel deflection, found its way into the back of the net. Subsequently, South Korea could not find their way back into the match.

The Uzbek miracle lived on. In the final, Akramov's side once again played a really exciting blend of attacking football and were the rightful winners, beating China 4-2. The subsequent celebrations inside the stadium were muted. Nobody had really expected to win. You could see the surprise expressions on the Uzbek players after the final whistle.

But on their return home, Uzbekistan were greeted by adulation from thousands of fans. The 1994 team became heroes and were celebrated many months after. This success, a first win at a major tournament, was supposed to herald a golden era of Uzbek football.

But three decades later, Uzbekistan have very much remained underdogs. The country hasn't won a major tournament since, and neither have Uzbekistan qualified for a World Cup at senior level.

In order to understand why football hasn't quite taken after 1994, you must understand Uzbekistan's history.

While part of the Soviet Union, Uzbekistan always benefitted from the Soviet infrastructure and funding. During the 1970s and '80s, the country had produced top players who would go on to represent the Soviet Union.

Post-independence there was a level of stagnation when it came to investment into football. At the time, the country fell under the dictatorship of Islam Karimov, who seized power immediately after independence in 1991 and remained in charge until his death.

Karimov created a harsh authoritarian state. During the 1990s, Karimov worked hard to eliminate all signs of opposition inside the country. Under him, Uzbekistan practised an isolationist foreign policy, which meant finances were finite. Football became of little importance to Karimov, and clubs became severely underfunded. Facilities became decrepit and run-down from the ravages of time. The domestic league dropped down in the rankings, and the standard of the competition gradually deteriorated.

This doesn't mean Uzbekistan were completely devoid of success. The country still produced top talent, who would go on to play at a high level in Europe, but never really fulfilled the potential that the 1994 Asian Games promised. Instead, the ensuing three decades can be summed up as one major disappointment – especially at international level for the senior national team.

'The chaos in the post-Soviet era turned into an anchor which held Uzbekistan and the other post-Soviet states back, while other nations such as South Korea, Japan and Saudi Arabia, who had previously not invested into football to the levels they began to in the late '90s, were able to accelerate ahead,' Conor Bowers, an expert in Uzbekistan football, explained.

But all of that changed with the death of Karimov in 2016. With his demise, Uzbekistan finally broke free of his dictatorship. In the post-Karimov era there has been newfound optimism, and a vibrant youthful society has been established. In 2024, around 60 per cent of Uzbekistan's population were under the age of 30, giving an enormous resource of young minds.

Nowhere have these changes been felt more acutely than in football. Freed from the shackles of Karimov's dictatorship, there is now new investment and structure within the Uzbek game spearheaded by people like former international player Odil Ahmedov, who became the vice-president of the Uzbekistan Football Association at the age of just 36 in 2021.

'It has really only been since Karimov's death that football in Uzbekistan has looked professional when compared to its contemporaries,' Bowers said.

In the years after Karimov, Uzbekistan has benefitted from new investment into the game, and has undergone a lot of restructuring as well. One of the major changes was the reduction in size of the top tier from 16 teams to only 12 in 2018. This has created a more competitive environment, which has in turn helped Uzbek clubs be more competitive in continental competitions like the AFC Champions League.

'Over the last two seasons, the competitiveness of the league has increased massively with teams like Nasaf, Navbahor, Neftchi and OGMK in particular able to compete against Pakhtakor and outplay and outperform them in many matches,' said Bowers.

The country's second division has also grown and developed as a result, pushing the competition even higher.

Bowers continued, 'Even within the Uzbek second tier [the ProLiga] in 2023 it contained two former league winners in Lokomotiv Tashkent [champions in 2018] and

Dinamo Samarqand [2016] and that league is as professional if not more than some of its central Asian neighbours.'

On top of restructuring the league, the Uzbekistan Football Association has also invested in building the infrastructure of football inside the country, including a state-of-the-art stadium in Tashkent – Milliy Stadium – which can host up to around 34,000 people, and cost £214m.

This has helped the country's young stars blossom, and has shifted Uzbekistan's mindset into football development and harnessing its exciting talent pool.

Bowers said, 'The recent focus on football development and improvements in infrastructure has allowed for youth players to have access to training and facilities which simply didn't exist outside of only a few teams such as Bunyodkor before. The Uzbekistan Football Association (UFA) introduced a requirement for teams to have youth teams as part of obtaining a professional licence, this in turn has created the introduction of under-21, under-19, etc. leagues, giving young players consistent youth football and a pathway to the first teams of their clubs.'

Another key figure behind the scenes alongside vice-president Ahmedov has been fellow former Uzbekistan international Timur Kapadze. Kapadze racked up over 100 caps and played in Russia and South Korea for many years during his career. He is the second-most capped player in Uzbekistan's history.

In 2021, Kapadze was appointed as head coach of the newly formed FK Olympic Tashkent. The club had been established by the country's Olympic committee with the goal of unifying the top talents within Uzbekistan.

Built solely on under-23 players, FK Olympic entered the second tier in the same year and earned promotion in their first season through the play-offs. Since then, they have remained in the top flight – where Kapadze has made them difficult to beat. They are financially well supported and have the backing of the Olympic committee to attract any potential top Uzbek talent to the club.

Gregg Britton, the former assistant manager of Uzbek top-flight side Sogdiana Jizzakh, has seen first-hand the developments inside the country, and he believes the appointment of Kapadze and the establishment of FK Olympic has made a huge difference in the evolution of Uzbek football.

'There's some really top minds and key people in the industry working for the federation at the moment,' Britton explained.

'One of them is Timor Kapadze. His education and understanding of football is excellent. I've done the [UEFA] pro licences with him, and he often goes to Europe to watch a few games and speak to people. He is educated on how players should be playing and what they should be doing. He's picked up on the European style and got away from the kick and rush football that some teams play in the league. He's set a new standard in the Super League. His style is technical and tactical, and it is very good.'

As well as managing FK Olympic, Kapadze has also been appointed to be in charge of Uzbekistan's under-23 and under-20 teams.

'They all train together so when they go into, say for instance, the Olympics or the under-20 competitions, they've already played quite a bit together through a full season or two seasons, so they should know the system and the way they want to play,' Britton said.

Meanwhile, regularly competing in senior football has also made the country's young stars able to better challenge at major youth international tournaments.

'In the 2022 season Olympic was notoriously hard to beat, even for teams like Pakhtakor and Navbahor. The use of senior men's football and the players playing together consistently allowed for the team to have a competitive advantage against other nations at the under-23 and youth Asian games competitions and make the later rounds,' Bowers said.

In the space of just two years Uzbekistan reaped the rewards of the Olympic programme. In 2023, Uzbekistan started the year by winning the under-20 Asian Cup hosted on home soil. Later that year they qualified for the under-20 World Cup, where they finished second behind Argentina in their group to qualify for the last 16. That proved a hurdle too far with Israel narrowly edging out Uzbekistan 1-0.

But it wasn't just the under-20 Uzbek team that enjoyed success at major competitions that year.

Uzbekistan also reached the semi-finals of the under-16 Asian Cup which saw them qualify for the under-17 World Cup in Indonesia. Pitted in a tough group with Spain and Mali, who would go on to win the bronze medal, Uzbekistan qualified to the last 16 after finishing in third place with four points – losing only to Mali, drawing with Spain in a 2-2 thriller and beating Canada. That set up a meeting with England's star-studded team, who had topped their group above Brazil and Iran. Miraculously, Uzbekistan stunned the young Three Lions and defeated them 2-1 to qualify for the quarter-finals for only the second time in the country's history. In the end, Uzbekistan were eliminated after a 1-0 defeat to France – but again the young stars had plenty to be proud of.

Uzbekistan's achievements for 2023 do not end there. In September of that year the under-23 team also won the bronze medal at the Asian Games, losing the semi-final to eventual champions South Korea and then thrashing Hong Kong 4-0 in the third-place match.

Kapadze and his Olympic players played a key role in the success of the under-20 and under-23 teams. What has been particularly impressive about Uzbekistan is that they haven't dropped deep and defended – but instead Kapadze's side have always looked to keep possession of the ball and play exciting attacking football, very much in line with the spirit of the 1994 team.

This has meant not just success on the pitch, but the opportunity to put players in the spotlight for scouts and agents. In the aftermath of these triumphs, the best-performing players at the tournament earned top moves abroad, including Abdukodir Khusanov who moved to Ligue 1 side RC Lens in the summer of 2023. Only 19 years old at the time, Khusanov went straight into the French club's first team and in the 2023/24 season he became only the seventh Uzbek player – also the youngest from his country – to appear in the Champions League. Impressively, he is also the first to accomplish this while playing for a west European club. The six others have represented Russian or other former Soviet clubs while playing in Europe's elite competition.

Khusanov was not alone. His fellow trailblazer, Abbosbek Fayzullaev, was named the Most Valuable Player at the under-20 Asian Cup and signed for CSKA Moscow, and also attracted plenty of interest from western European clubs as well.

Together the two of them have trodden a completely new path for young Uzbek footballers. In the country's history, few have ventured out into western Europe and have enjoyed success. But there is hope that Fayzullaev and Khusanov can finally buck that trend.

Others from Uzbekistan have started to make similar moves. In 2024, Brentford signed 18-year-old Uzbek youth international Mukhammadali Urinboev to their B team. Urinboev became the first Uzbek player to sign for a Premier League club. Undoubtedly, this has been another significant leap in the trajectory of the country – and one that is proof that more and more scouts are exploring the region.

'Their infrastructure is slowly coming through, and the money's been put in slowly, but they've always had raw talent and it's trying to put that raw talent into perspective,' Gregg Britton explained.

'Like I say, they've always had that. But it's trying to put that towards developing even further from there, so it's always good having one or two players or six players, but you need to have a squad at the end of the day to start performing. And slowly but surely, that's what's happening now.'

Britton also believed the impact of Khusanov and others doing well had the potential to create a snowball effect, 'They [Uzbek players] should be given these opportunities or can be given these opportunities, but again I'm just guessing partly it might be down to the fact that they're scared. Scared to be the first or second player to actually go abroad to western Europe and try it? Khusanov is a great example, now playing in the Champions League.

'So if he can keep playing well as one of the first ones to do it. Maybe others could turn around and say, "If he could do it, I could do it," and anyone else could do it. So other players need to sort of try it out and give these opportunities a go to see how they feel.'

Another key development that could give Uzbek players more exposure and spotlight is the expansion of the World Cup. One of the biggest beneficiaries of the finals increasing from 32 to 48 teams from 2026 onwards are Asian countries.

The AFC will have a possible maximum of nine representatives in 2026 – which is almost double in size compared to the previous maximum they could have at the 2022 tournament, excluding the hosts.

This gives countries like Uzbekistan a real shot at qualification. At the Asian Cup in 2023, they easily reached the quarter-finals. They only lost out to eventual winners Qatar in a penalty shoot-out. If they can continue in a similar fashion during the qualifying process for the 2026 World Cup, Uzbekistan will have every chance of reaching a long-sought World Cup, and the country's young stars will get an opportunity to try to emulate their feats from youth tournaments at senior international level as well.

'For me this is now possibly the start of some of these younger players, like Fayzullaev and Khusanov, who are already playing in the senior national team at the Asian Cup. They've come from that sort of background [achieving success at youth international tournaments] and their era of where they're playing,' said Britton.

'Like I say there's going to be many, many other players as well for me, that will carry on and go into that senior setup eventually. And I'm hoping that they do make the next FIFA World Cup, they've got a real chance.'

With so much resurgence and evolution in the game in Uzbekistan, it's no surprise to see how the country has almost exploded during the beginning of the 2020s and has started to finally build on the success of the 1994 team. In the coming years, this new generation will look to write even more history, and begin an exciting new era in Uzbek football.

# 22

# American Samoa

THOMAS RONGEN was sitting in a bar with a friend. He was already a couple of pints in when his phone rang. It was his boss, Sunil Gulati, on the other line. Little did Rongen know it at the time, but that phone call would change the rest of his life, and American Samoan football for ever.

At the time, Rongen was enjoying his downtime having successfully accomplished his job with the USA under-20 team, taking them to qualification for the World Cup. He was looking forward to sitting back and relaxing for the next couple of months. But fate, or more specifically Gulati, had other plans for the Dutch coach.

'He told me he knows I got some spare time and that there was an enclave of the United States called American Samoa, who were looking for some help for a few weeks on the technical side,' Rongen recalled.

Rongen's first reaction was to Google American Samoa and to find it on a map. 'I've never been to that part of the world,' he said. 'So based on that, not knowing anything about American Samoa, I said yes.'

A few more Google searches and pints later, Rongen discovered he was about to coach the worst country according to FIFA rankings at the time. A team who had not won a single game in its history. A team who had not scored a goal in 20 years. But instead of regretting his decision, he was even more buoyed by the prospect.

'That was even more of a reason for me to not only discover a new country, a new culture, but more so to do something we as Dutch like – taking on impossible tasks. I look at most things as challenges not as obstacles, so I was really looking forward to it,' Rongen said.

Even so, Rongen had no idea just how impossible of a task he had signed up for at the time. Almost a decade prior to Rongen's arrival on the island, American Samoa suffered the country's most historically humiliating defeat. In 2002, they had faced Australia in a World Cup qualifier. Just prior to the game, most of American Samoa's players found out they were ineligible to feature because American Samoa was an unincorporated territory of the United States, bordering the far-bigger Samoan islands. Most of the players in American Samoa's squad possessed Samoan passports, rather than American Samoan US-issued passports. Samoa, however, is a sovereign nation of its own. This meant American Samoa had to field a team largely made up of teenagers against an Australian side full of professional senior players playing at the top of their game.

The fixture would go down in history. American Samoa's goalkeeper, Nicky Salapu, would be haunted by it for years to come. He'd have vivid nightmares of Australia's goals pouring in past him like torrential rain, one minute after another in an endless barrage, conceding 31 times.

Australia's 31-0 victory became a world record, which has stood the test of time for the ensuing two decades and more. Salapu spent the next few years replaying that game on his Xbox console – scoring as many past Australia as he could in a bid to avenge that fateful and humiliating defeat.

But Rongen arrived on the island in 2011 to change all of that. He wanted to give the American Samoa players a new lease of life and help them accomplish something they had never done before.

Just how big of a challenge he was about to undertake hit him even before he stepped a foot in American Samoa.

Rongen recalled, 'I spoke to the president literally two days before I left, and I remember him telling me that they only had about five decent soccer balls on the whole island.'

Fortunately, Rongen was under contract with Nike, who shipped not just footballs but other equipment to help him coach achieve his ambitions.

There were other challenges as well. Rongen had been to every continent on the planet. He had travelled far and wide both in his personal and professional life. But he had never quite experienced anywhere like American Samoa.

'It was like walking into a time warp,' he said. 'I grew up in the late 1960s, and '70s. I encountered third-world countries during my travels even then with the Dutch Olympic team that were way behind in soccer for a lot of reasons, but you could see this was a country who were very much down at the bottom.'

American Samoa lacked resources and funding. As well as not having enough footballs, there was a scarcity in kit supplies, cones and other paraphernalia. On top of that, there were few places on the island that were even fit to play football on.

It became obvious very early on that Rongen's immediate challenges were nothing like the ones he had been accustomed to in his professional career working in the MLS or with the USA national team.

To coach American Samoa, Rongen had to get back to the very basics of the sport. To begin with he had to get his team in shape, not just physically but mentally as well.

He recalled, 'I did a lot of research and had a lot of their previous games sent to me. For about a month before

I travelled to American Samoa I studied those games, and at the end what I discovered was that this team was not a 31-nothing team. I also looked at games against our other opponents, where they [American Samoa] would lose ten, 12 or 14 goals to nothing. Anything under ten was like a victory for them.'

For years American Samoa's team had been battered over and over again, not just in the physical sense on the pitch but mentally as well. The challenge for Rongen, therefore, was to figure out a way to pick them up. But how do you do that to a team who are ranked bottom of the world, and who haven't won a single game in their entire competitive history?

Rongen said, 'I knew that I could close that gap quite rapidly. To begin with you could tell that they weren't fit enough. But I knew if I'd tweak some things tactically that we could make great strides.

'It's very hard in three weeks to make players technically a lot better, but I definitely set my goal to help them in that area as well. However, the most important part of the four components, from the physical, technical, tactical became the mental part. Without a doubt.'

Rongen found a team lacking spirit and belief. A team that was in some ways divided as well. He only had a few weeks before American Samoa's 2014 World Cup qualifiers but in that time most of his energy was invested in creating team unity.

'I did a lot of team building both on the field but more so off the field,' Rongen explained.

'We put in a lot of work in order to heal scars and in order to eventually get a group with a losing mentality to a group that at least thought they had a chance in the games ahead.'

One of Rongen's first decisions was to bring Nicky Salapu back to the national team environment. Still very much haunted by what had happened against Australia all those years ago, Salapu had retired years prior, but his unexpected return gave American Samoa a new incentive to right the wrongs of the country's past.

'The catalyst for me was that I brought the goalkeeper back who had retired,' explained Rongen. 'He was the one who gave up 31 goals and told me that "my son thinks I'm a loser because people recognise me in the streets and say, oh, you're the guy that conceded 31 goals". I convinced him to come back so we had a real rallying cry, you know, when he arrived to do it for Nicky.'

Rongen was also determined to break the cultural divide between his players. At the time American Samoa was an island divided into several tribes. From speaking to former players in the national team ahead of his arrival, Rongen realised that these tribes didn't always get along with each other, 'I also knew that there were some tribal issues and at certain tribes in the islands there, several tribes are bigger, stronger and more dominant, and you see that back in society, but also in football. The dominant players were from the bigger tribes. But they weren't necessarily the better players.'

Rongen, however, knew if his team was going to be successful, he needed unity among his squad. He needed players ready to collaborate and work with each other. So, he did his best to make sure new bonds were formed and tried to break down the cultural barriers as best as he could within the space of just a few weeks. This involved an intense programme in which Rongen moved all of his players into the same building to cohabit ahead of the World Cup qualifiers.

He said, 'I broke it up a little bit by attaching those dominant players to players from other tribes as well. I also put us in a camp, which was unbelievable. I slept there myself.

We were in this three-storey, Spartan-like building, a little bit of water was still in there. I told everybody we're going to be here for ten days and we're going to train twice a day.'

This would become a gruelling regime for Rongen's players, who were mostly part-time and spent their day jobs in tuna factories and fishing boats before going back to their commune and training in the mornings and evenings.

'I would drive the guys at 6am to their boats,' Rongen explained. 'About 80 per cent worked hard labour on tuna boats. Tuna is their biggest industry. I would pick them up at 9.30, and you could tell these guys were exhausted. We would train for two hours. Bring them back to their tuna plants where they would stand on a belt, you know, put a tube on a can or whatever. Then back to practise at 4pm.'

After training sessions in the evenings, Rongen would get his team to participate in problem-solving exercises to create even more cohesion among them.

Rongen recalled, 'We all basically slept on blankets on the floor. There were free rooms on every storey in the building and I was able to separate the dominant groups based on positions, so I had the centre-backs live in one room, etc. Each and every night they had to come up with an answer to a question and to solve a problem technically and tactically within their position, which made them communicate with each other, which also made them communicate with other tribes they didn't particularly care for. They also realised we're all in the same boat, you know? Let's do this.'

Another key factor why Rongen was able to succeed and relate to his players was because he embraced the culture. American Samoa was a deeply religious country, and full of unique customs. Rongen not only attended church with his players, but he very quickly accepted the team's transgender player Jaiyah Saelua, something previous coaches who had travelled to the island had not been able to do.

He said, 'I heard they [the previous coaches] never really accepted their culture, including not embracing Jaiyah, who comes from the Polynesian fa'afafine culture, which is third gender, and is very normal in their society. It's also something a Dutchman is not shocked by and will embrace as well.'

In return for embracing the American Samoan culture, Rongen received his own sort of spiritual awakening as well, which helped him to heal from the tragic loss of his daughter seven years prior in a single-car accident.

'For me, my journey was letting go of all my guilt of my daughter. And if it wasn't for these beautiful people on this island, through their religion, through their openness towards others, they probably saved my life from a personal standpoint and it was just an incredible experience for me that made me, not religious, but certainly more, more spiritual,' he said.

Throughout his time on the island, Rongen created a tight family unit. He even stood up for his players against the country's federation, demanding better organisation and more money for their travels, 'The players are afraid of the the president and the CEO because they can make or break those guys at a whim, which happened in the past, so I picked a fight about a scheduling conflict that had to do with going to church.

'I wanted this group to know by fighting the establishment that I am behind them. So that was a huge moment. Afterwards, I heard them talk on the field and say stuff like, "Oh my God, he's the first coach that ever, you know went after a president and fought for us." So that was a huge moment.'

Rongen also worked on the physical side of the game. He inherited a team who were not match-fit when he arrived on the island. Most of the squad were there to make up the numbers. Several of his team members were overweight.

'I knew I really only had 14 players who could compete at this level,' he acknowledged. 'The others were there if there would have been an injury in more of a supporting role.'

Rongen worked his tactics around that, utilising the players whom he saw the most potential in and working his way around them to find the best system, 'I modified tactically how we were going to play. I played the Dutch style. I also saw that the other teams we were going to face had a very passive high line defensively. So I knew that if we were smart, I had a good passer, I had a great passing centre-back, I had a great passing midfielder. I had Nicky in goal and a number nine that can blow everybody's doors off. So in my axis I had the best players. And I knew that if we would be smart in our runs, that we would have three or four one vs ones with the goalkeepers due to the effect of the passive high line of the opposing teams.'

That was a tactical setup that Rongen was able to implement gradually, starting in small groups and eventually training 11 vs 11. But in order to achieve it, he knew his team had to improve physically as well. Rongen's gruelling regime to train twice a day was part of that process to get them into better shape. Even on their days off, Rongen wouldn't rest. As part of his team-building exercises, he would take his players on hikes around the island, including climbing the summit of Lata Mountain – the tallest peak in American Samoa.

He said, 'Off the field I wanted them to overcome things that people thought couldn't be done. I picked the highest mountain on the islands, and I said we're going to go to the peak and climb up the biggest electric construction built on top of it, which only three people in the island had ever done, so I wanted them to conquer that.'

Rongen gathered his entire squad to participate in the hike, including himself. The weather on the day was humid. Rongen remembered stifling conditions and most of his players struggling through the many hours it took to climb the peak. It was something that not all of his players enjoyed, but it was another part of the process that Rongen believed created more unity within his squad, 'I would partake in all of those things myself to show them the way basically. It took us hours to get there, and we were exhausted. That showed us again that we can do this together if we're organised.

'It taught them to help their weaker players because we had, you know, exceptional physical players, but we also had some guys that were a little bit overweight. The more fitter and better players were able to push their weaker players up. The whole thing taught us that we're only as good as our weakest link. So it not only made the top players of the island better, but it also made sure the rest of the 12–14 players in the squad also became better and stronger during the process.'

Everything Rongen had planned had a meaning behind it. There was a military-like precision to the way he coached his players and prepared them for what would be a historic World Cup qualification process for the country.

On the last day, before the team was set to travel to neighbouring Samoa where the qualification fixtures would take place, Rongen took his players to Breakers Point at the summit of Papatele Ridge. This was the point that provided the base for the American Samoan army to protect itself during a Tongan invasion in the 20th century. Standing next to the cannon, Rongen gave a rousing speech about its historic significance, which he admittedly fabricated a 'little bit' by turning it into a David and Goliath story about the smaller American Samoan army fending off the giant enemy. If they noticed the exaggerated story, none of his players pointed it out but instead joined in on Rongen's rallying cries. By that point Rongen had made his team believe. They had become enchanted with his ways.

He said, 'It was this big fucking cannon. So, everybody ended up sitting on the cannon and yes, I fabricated the story a little bit and turned it into a real emotional plight. I told them your forefathers were able to do this with a smaller army so there's no way when we have equal numbers we can let them beat us. Eventually, I got them to a point where they believed they could beat Tonga, but a lot of blood, sweating and tears went into that.'

His team set off the following day. This wasn't a glorious trip with chartered private aeroplanes. Neither were they greeted with luxury hotels in neighbouring Samoa. When Rongen's team walked out to face Tonga in their opening fixture there were only a few dozen spectators in attendance.

Set in the heart of the rainforest in Apia, the national stadium of Samoa boasts merely a tiny, covered stand provided mostly for visiting dignitaries. It wasn't exactly the setting of a Hollywood story. Before the game, even Rongen had his doubts about whether his team's hard work would result in a significant change in their performance or whether all of their efforts would have been in vain. After all, he was coaching what was officially the worst team in the world. The worst team in the world who had never won a single game in the country's history.

But all of his doubts evaporated as he gave his final rousing speech in the lead-up to the game, and he saw the determination in his players, 'My wife was with me on the day that we played Tonga. I walked out of that meeting when I announced the starting XI. I saw it in their eyes, and I said to my wife walking out, I think they feel they can be victorious. That was a huge accomplishment for me to be able to make them believe in such a short amount of time.'

On 22 November 2011 as American Samoa kicked off against Tonga in the early 3pm start on a random Tuesday, for the first time in the country's history not everyone expected to lose.

At first there were no signs of a remarkable upset being on the cards. The game began with both sides trying to feel each other out. Tonga had tested Nicky Salapu in goal several times but could not find a way through. As the minutes ticked on and Rongen screamed on from the sidelines, you could tell there was a bit of frustration growing within the much-favoured Tongans. Nobody wanted to lose to the worst team in the world after all.

Frustration was exactly what Rongen had planned to create. American Samoa had been instructed to keep the ball, and to defend resolutely. This was the kind of opponent Tonga had not expected to come up against.

The real shock of the first half came towards the end, when Ramin Ott, an American Samoan US soldier, took a long-range shot at the Tongan goal. It was a well-hit strike that seemed to take the goalkeeper by surprise. The ball bounced just in front of him and then deflected from his head into the back of the net. Ott raced towards Rongen on the touchline and the rest of his team-mates followed. Just by scoring the first goal the American Samoa team had done something they had never done in their history – take the lead in a competitive match.

During the half-time break Rongen tried to manage the emotions. All the mental preparation going into the game helped American Samoa keep their mettle in the second half. Rongen's men controlled possession, continuing to frustrate the Tongans. As the minutes ticked by you could see the sweat perspiring more on the Tongan heads in the humid Samoan heat. Rongen's team only grew more in confidence.

With 15 minutes to go, Rongen's secret weapon, Shalom Luani – whose electrifying speed American Samoa tried to utilise – raced through one vs one on the Tongan goal. The ball bounced up into the air as the goalkeeper rushed out. Luani, who would go on to play in the NFL, was too quick, and got a toe to poke the ball into the back of the net before colliding with the goalkeeper.

There were whistles and cheers in the crowd as the players rushed towards Luani writhing on the floor. Rongen, though, remained resolute on the sidelines, eager not to get too carried away.

In the ensuing minutes Tonga rushed forward desperately trying to avoid the upset. But American Samoa were too determined not to let the game slip. In the last ten minutes of the game Rongen's side were fighting for their life, putting their bodies on the line. Tonga managed to get one past Salapu in the 88th minute, but American Samoa held on.

The emotions were palpable on the pitch as the final whistle blew. At first it seemed like the American Samoans didn't quite know how to react. But then Salapu fell on his knees and looked up at the sky and Rongen rushed towards his players. Minutes later they were performing a celebration dance, called the *siva tau*.

Rongen said, 'It was brilliant. A brilliant experience for me, but more so for those players that really are amateurs and just want to come out and make their country proud, which they weren't able to do for 20 years. They were the laughing stock among the American football players and the rugby players that had some success.

'And eventually, when they succeeded to make their country proud, that was just a great moment for that group, and also for soccer in general in the country in terms of acceptance, recognition and respect from other athletes towards them.'

That victory alone was enough for Rongen's team to write themselves into the history books. But inside the dressing room, the players were on cloud nine and wanted to aim for even more. Rongen didn't just make his team believe they could win one game, he also made them believe that they could win over and over again.

The preliminary World Cup qualification consisted of not just American Samoa and Tonga, but also the Cook Islands and Samoa; the latter had won their game 3-2. Only the top team would qualify for the next round of Oceania's World Cup qualification.

Up next for American Samoa were the Cook Islands. They had lost their first game against Samoa, but only narrowly in the dying embers thanks to a dramatic 91st-minute winner. They knew anything but a win against American Samoa would all but eliminate their chances of qualification into the next round.

Rongen knew this was going to be another tough test. But again, his team rose to the challenge. Luani, the scorer of American Samoa's second goal in the first game, again proved the key. Just 48 hours after that historic first victory, he broke through the Cook Islands' defence after 25 minutes and slotted the ball into the back of the net before raising his arms in the air and rushing off to celebrate with his team-mates. American Samoa were really starting to get into the groove of things now. Unlike when they took the lead against Tonga, the celebrations were less palpable and more relaxed. Rongen's men were enjoying themselves for probably one of the first times in their lives while playing a competitive international fixture.

American Samoa pretty much controlled the rest of the game. It was only thanks to an unfortunate set piece which saw Tala Luvu head into his own net that the Cook Islands equalised. After the final whistle there was disappointment on the faces of some of the American Samoan players. This was a team who had lost the vast majority of their games in their entire history. Here they were needing just one more win in their final match to win the group. This was a chance they would have all bitten their hands off to make a reality before they arrived at the qualifying process, and yet there was a level of disappointment. It's amazing what difference the space of 48 hours can make. What difference one result can make to transform the perspective of an entire nation, and group of players.

In the final game, Rongen's men were up against their neighbours, Samoa. Both teams needed a victory to qualify for the next round. Samoa had beaten the Cook Islands, but they had drawn with Tonga in their second game.

This was essentially a final. On the day of the match the elements had changed. Whereas American Samoa were bathed in sunshine in their draw with the Cook Islands two days prior, there were now grey clouds floating in the sky. Rain had swept the ground and made it into a muddy, bobbly surface.

The conditions meant the game turned into a scrappy mess with loose touches and rash challenges. Both teams were determined to win, and Rongen's players gave it their all. There were no signs that this was the worst-ranked team in football as the American Samoans fought to seize control of the match. They rode their luck at times but had chances to take the lead. Nicky Salapu and the Samoan goalkeeper both had to make some crucial saves in order to keep the game 0-0 until the final minutes.

Then in the final minute American Samoa broke through on goal. For a brief flickering moment it seemed like they were going to do it. The ball flew past the helpless Samoan goalkeeper. It seemed like there was only one place it was heading towards – the back of the net. But then it bobbled on the muddy surface and deflected on to the post. Samoa had survived. The American Samoans held their heads in their hands. They had come inches away from doing something they could not even have imagined in their wildest dreams. But the game was not over. Samoa took control of the ball and tried to create one last chance of their own. Taking advantage of American Samoa's disorientation, they found a way through on the counterattack. Salapu rushed out to meet the onrushing opponent, but he slipped the ball through the goalkeeper's legs and into the back of the net.

The groans of the American Samoans echoed around the stands. Rongen's men had given it their all but in the end it wasn't enough. The American Samoans looked crushed on the pitch. There were tears and sunken heads after the final whistle. Rongen, though, didn't let that final moment define what the American Samoans had achieved. He picked up every single player after the final whistle.

He recalled, 'We were their equals against Samoa. If we scored that last chance [which ended up hitting the post], then we would have gone to the final stage. But instead, they go on the counter and score to make it one to nothing.

'It was that close, and it shows we clearly became more competitive across the board against teams that I felt were equal or only a little bit better, not 20 goals better.'

Rongen has remained adamant that his time coaching on the island was his most profound experience in the game.

'I won an MLS Cup, two trophies as a coach, two trophies as a player but this was the most rewarding personal and professional experience without a doubt,' he said.

In American Samoa, Rongen was able to rediscover his passion for the game. His players gave him the hope and faith that he had lost in the hyper-commercialised product which football had become in the western world – the product which fixates on results, and which drives managers to unimaginable levels of pressure where every win feels like a relief and every loss like a crushing blow that is going to swallow you up.

Rongen said, 'We are so focused on greatness and things like that. Sports is just getting out of control. That's what draws me towards the amateurs doing their country proud. It's a reminder of how spiritual and simple football is. We all fall in love with football at five, six or seven years old because it is just beautiful, you know. We fall in love with what it means to kick a ball around simply for the love of the person you're kicking the ball to. I think that they [American Samoa] are an incredible case in point. I definitely rediscovered the love for this game due to these people.'

Rongen left the island after the qualification process to return to the US. However, he has been back since helping to provide coaching courses in American Samoa to develop the game. The foundations he has put in place remained even after his departure. During 2018 World Cup qualifying, American Samoa managed to record two wins and missed out on top place in the group on goal difference by one goal. After scoring just six competitive goals in a decade between 2000 and 2010 and losing every single game, American Samoa almost doubled that from 2010 to 2020, scoring 11 goals, winning three times and drawing twice. Rongen started a process in American Samoa which has inspired others to take up football and to continue to develop the game.

'You don't go somewhere to leave a legacy, but I remember after I left and I spoke to the president many months and years later, that soccer had become the second-most popular sport on the island. It had surpassed American football. There were more participants, more girls started to play, there were more referee courses, and they built two more soccer fields,' Rongen says.

'We jumped 30 places I think in FIFA [rankings] so my legacy there is, as the president explained to me, 'Thomas, what you have done for this country, we know we haven't caught up with the rest of the world yet, but we finally feel for the first time that we are starting to see an incredible amount of progress." Outside of my personal and professional experiences it's nice to look back at that and see that you've made a difference somewhere in the world.'

It's a legacy which has also been documented and turned into a Hollywood movie called *Next Goal Wins*, directed by Oscar-winner Taika Waititi and released in 2023. The film is a work of fiction which often distorts the reality of Rongen and American Samoa's story. But it's an inspiring tale which captures the essence of Rongen's work on the island.

Looking ahead, it's difficult to predict what the future of football holds in American Samoa. Even though Rongen and many others have now made great strides to develop the game, there are still barriers that have to be overcome.

'Yes, there's money from FIFA, but it doesn't always end up where it needs to end up,' Rongen said. 'I've been back twice to put a course on for ten days to get better coaches, you know, into American Samoa to raise the level of training sessions and eventually games as well and that's a slow process because they're devoid of resources.'

There are other limitations from a geographical point of view that also hold American Samoa back from truly raising the game in the country.

Rongen continued, 'Let's be real honest, we are talking about these tiny islands in the middle of nowhere. So, it's not like next week, let's play a friendly, we're driving half an hour down the road. Every time they want to play a game, a friendly game, exhibition game or practice games, they have to get on a plane, and unfortunately finances prohibit them getting a lot of quality games.'

But that doesn't mean things are not heading in the right direction. Rongen's influence has seen the game evolve. American Samoa has established its own league, and there are now clubs competing in the OFC Champions League as well.

He said, 'Because of the increased level of interest in the game, there is an adult league. There's a youth league as well, where they play eight months of the year, every Saturday. Some teams train once or twice a week due to greater facilities. Others are only playing on the fields where it's very hard to hone your technical and tactical skills because the conditions are so poor.'

The reality is that the gap between Oceania and the rest of the world is still an enormous abyss. American Samoa will likely always be outside the periphery of the world's game.

'These countries will continue to struggle. I think going forward due to their isolation and due to the fact that other sports are more dominant so that's where most government money goes,' said Rongen.

'And what FIFA gives these countries is a pittance in order to catch up with the rest of the world, or in order to catch up just within Oceania. To eventually maybe have a chance to go to the World Cup, I don't think that will ever happen in my lifetime or will ever happen in the history going forward, unfortunately for those countries that are fighting those battles each and every day.'

American Samoans will likely understand the situation they are in. But that doesn't mean the game cannot evolve or there is no point in helping to advance football in the region. After all, football is more than just a game about qualifying for the big events and winning trophies. It's about the experiences and the moments that happen along the way. It's about that goal that you scored to write yourself into the history books. It's about that victory that made the whole country believe and celebrate in ecstasy. That is why everyone loves an underdog like American Samoa – not only for what they achieved but for the memories they have created along the way.

# 23

# Brentford

THOMAS FRANK pumped his fists in the air and bathed in the Wembley sunshine. Around him his players were embracing each other in gleaming smiles. For the last two years the club had done everything to get to where they wanted to be. With setbacks and crushing defeats along the way, Frank had finally done it. For the first time in 74 years Brentford had been promoted to the top flight of English football. They had beaten Swansea in the play-off final, and they were heading to the Premier League.

What Brentford achieved in the summer of 2021 is something few would have even fathomed a decade earlier. Ten years prior, Brentford were languishing in mid-table in the third tier. For much of their history Brentford had ebbed and flowed like the tides of the ocean. They had wandered back and forth between the fourth, the third and occasionally the second levels. Reaching the top flight seemed like an elusive dream, especially during the beginning of the 21st century.

Brentford were founded in 1889, three years prior to the foundation of England's most successful club, Liverpool, and six years before Chelsea were established. Historically Brentford had always been a household name in English football but never the juggernaut they have gone on to become.

Instead, Brentford enjoyed relative success, reaching a peak during the 1930s, and even finishing a historic fifth place in the First Division. During the pre-Second World War years, Brentford spent four consecutive seasons in the top flight which was the pinnacle of their achievements during the 20th century. In the postwar era, their fortunes declined. In the first season after the war in 1946/47, Brentford were relegated to the second tier.

Brentford would struggle to return to the top level for the ensuing 74 years. The years that followed saw Brentford relegated even further, to the third tier by the 1950s. The club would incur financial problems, and in the decades ahead it would be on the brink of collapse several times. By the 1960s, Brentford would sink even further down, to the bottom division. They would spend the 1970s and '80s bouncing back and forth between the two divisions.

In the 1990s, there was a brief revival when Brentford managed to reach the second tier for the 1992/93 season, but they would finish 22nd and would be relegated back to the third tier.

During those decades, Brentford's financial problems meant they always had to operate on meagre budgets and sometimes beyond their means. On several occasions the club came close to the brink of collapse again.

The height of Brentford's financial problems came during the early 2000s. At the time the sale of Darren Powell to Crystal Palace eventually rescued the club from administration. However, by then it was obvious something had to change. Someone had to find a more sustainable solution for the longevity of the club.

Along came Matthew Benham, a wealthy businessman and a lifelong Brentford fan. Benham was a Physics graduate from the University of Oxford. He had made his fortune thanks to his gambling consultancy firm, Smartodds. He was devoted to changing things around at the club, and steadily began to invest his money. This gradually led to Benham taking full control in 2012.

Coming from a background of betting and data, Benham wanted to instil his own method. Like many he had realised the potential of data in football, which at the time was still being extremely underutilised in the sport, especially in comparisons to other major sports in the United States. Benham was keen to build a culture at Brentford which was similar to that of Billy Beane's *Moneyball* movement in baseball. It was made famous by the Hollywood movie of the same name where Brad Pitt portrayed a determined Beane who teamed up with a maths whizz Yale graduate, portrayed by Jonah Hill, to transform the fortunes of the Oakland Athletics by recruiting players based on data. The truth was not far from the fiction. Beane's revolutionary movement transformed baseball and inspired a generation in the sport taking the Oakland Athletics to new heights.

By the early 2010s, this data-led movement was also starting to emerge in football. Benham was one of the first people taking up senior roles in the sport who decided on this approach. To do this Benham recruited data-minded people who he had worked with at Smartodds, including Phil Giles who eventually ended up becoming the director of football at Brentford.

Immediately, just like Beane did with the Oakland Athletics, Brentford sought out undervalued targets in the transfer market. During the first few years under Benham, Brentford brought in the likes of Will Grigg from Walsall and Andre Gray from Luton Town – both were later sold for mass profits, the latter ending up at Premier League club Burnley.

Benham's investment and change in policy brought almost immediate success. Brentford became much more competitive in League One and earned promotion to the Championship in the 2013/14 season for the first time in 21 years.

Over the following years Benham's strategy saw Brentford become a stable team in England's second tier, and gradually turn more and more competitive. With better performances came more profit and even better acquisitions.

One of Brentford's best signings in the new Benham era was a young French centre-forward in Neal Maupay, who arrived at the club in 2017. Maupay had scored 11 goals in France's second tier the previous season, but the data suggested he had the potential to become even more prolific. In his first season, Maupay went on to make 17 goal contributions for Brentford, before going on to make 33 goal contributions in his second season and being sold to Premier League club Brighton & Hove Albion for a huge profit.

Maupay wasn't Brentford's only masterstroke; in 2017 they also signed Ollie Watkins from Exeter City. Only 21 years old at the time, Watkins had scored 13 goals in League Two during the 2016/17 season. But the data showed there was potential for more. Watkins was a versatile attacking player, capable of playing on the wings and centrally as well. In his first season, Watkins made 15 goal contributions in the Championship for Brentford. He followed that up with 19 goal contributions in his second season.

But Brentford didn't just recruit players well. Benham and his team also brought in the right personnel to work alongside them. One of Brentford's most important recruitments was bringing in Thomas Frank. The Dane had spent three years overachieving in Denmark's top flight with Brøndby IF and he initially arrived in 2016 as an assistant manager under Dean Smith. Frank quickly embraced Brentford's methods and championed the club's idea of data recruitment. He was vital in establishing exciting attacking football and making Brentford better in the Championship. When Smith left to join Aston Villa in October 2018, Brentford had the obvious candidate primed and ready and promoted Frank from within.

Frank's initial period in charge would begin with rocky foundations, winning just one of his first ten games. But Brentford persisted with Frank despite pressures from some sections of their supporters. The underlying data had shown Frank's side was actually underperforming based on expected goals and other key metrics.

Brentford's faith paid off. In January 2019, Frank collected seven points from a possible nine and was nominated for Championship Manager of the Month award. He switched to a back three, and used an innovative 3-4-3 system, which exploited the flanks and created a really exciting attacking side.

Tactics-wise, he was able to get the best out of Brentford, and soon his team were showing the form that the underlying data had suggested was always there from the beginning of Frank's time as manager.

It wasn't just Frank's ability to establish tactics that worked on the pitch. He was also a brilliant man-manager, who was always able to deal with setbacks and new characters in the team. As he grew into his role, Frank was able to handle departures of key players from his squad on a regular basis. In fact, he was able to make Brentford better, even after losing key players, and was able to maintain high morale and constantly inspire his players to improve and reach new heights.

One of the first significant moments was having to replace Neal Maupay in 2019. Maupay was Brentford's star player in the previous season. But when he left for Brighton, his departure rocked the club. Maupay was a fan favourite and a key player in the dressing room. However, Frank wasn't fazed. Instead, he decided to promote Watkins into the centre-forward role and make him the focal point of the attack, something the club's scouts had identified was a possibility when they initially scouted the player at Exeter.

'When we looked at him from Exeter, he was mostly playing as a ten. So, if you're in there, then you are close to being a striker and the way we want to play we would like to have wingers who think like strikers and arrive in the box,' Frank explained.

'You can also see two of the best goalscorers in the world – Ronaldo and Messi both started as wingers, so I think the more of my players that can think like a striker, even the centre-backs when there is a set piece, I think that's the key.

'To be fair already under Dean [Smith] he tried him a few times as a striker. So, I thought he looked good there. We knew it was in the bank when I took over. And then when Neal [Maupay] left, we got the opportunity.'

Frank, though, had to first get Watkins onboard. Having seen Maupay depart for pastures new, Watkins was uncertain about his future. He was already being pursued by Premier League clubs, and the temptation to follow Maupay's progress was something Frank had to dissuade him from.

Frank said in a 2021 press conference, after Watkins had been called up to the England squad, 'I clearly remember when I sat down with him and my assistant head coach, Brian Riemer, during the pre-season camp for last season where he was considering whether he should go or not go. I said, "No, if you need to leave this club, you need to leave it on a high and so we'll play you as a striker and we will develop you to do that. And then when you leave this club, you finished on a high." When you finish on a high, become the top scorer of the league, named the best player of the league and all that, it's easier to take the next step. Not easy but easier and he did that, and the rest is history.'

Frank's ability to persuade Watkins worked a charm. He finished the 2019/20 season with 25 goals in the Championship and was voted the EFL Championship Player of the Year. Watkins's goals also helped Brentford to the play-off final at Wembley, although even he was not enough to help Frank's side reach the top flight. Brentford lost to Fulham in extra time, and Watkins left to join Aston Villa in the Premier League a month later. A few months later he made his debut for the senior England team, and the rest is history.

After that crushing defeat at Wembley, Brentford didn't just lose Watkins, but they also sold Saïd Benrahma, who had made 27 goal contributions for the club during the previous season. Without Benrahma and Watkins, Frank again had a lot of work to do to get morale back up. Not only did he have to replace their incredible output, but the Dane had to motivate his players to go again, and once more data was used. Brentford's directors had shown the players that the underlying data suggested they were the better side against Fulham at Wembley, and that they had the potential to perform even better in the Championship during the following season.

To replace Watkins, Brentford signed Ivan Toney, a striker who had made 30 goal contributions in 32 games in League One during the previous season. Frank also retained Bryan Mbeumo – who they had signed as a 19-year-old from France during the previous season. Mbeumo only made 13 goal contributions in his last season in Ligue 2 but in his first season he contributed with 24 for Brentford.

Together with Mbeumo, Toney would play a key role in firing Brentford to the Premier League. In total Toney contributed with a whopping 43 goal contributions in 53 games for Frank's side. With 31 goals in the Championship, Toney set a record in the division for the most goals scored in a single season.

Remarkably, despite losing Maupay and Watkins, Brentford became a better team with Toney in the side.

'You know the problem is if I tell you the secret, it's not a secret any more,' Frank answered when I asked him about the secret recipe behind Brentford's success in 2021.

'To answer your question, the secret is there's no secret. I think we try to work with them individually. Both as players and as a person and try to get the team performing. So, we've been good at that. Luckily. Maybe we can't continue that, but let's hope.'

Even though there were distinct differences to the style of play employed by Watkins and Toney, Frank's system at Brentford was able to accommodate both of their approaches and bring out the best of them.

'About Ollie [Watkins] and Ivan [Toney]. Both of them are really good to arrive in the box and in the right areas and that's a key thing to score your main goals in and around the six-yard box, but definitely inside the 18-yard box,' said Frank.

'I think that maybe Ollie has got a tiny bit more pace and runs a little bit more in behind [the opposition's defence] and Ivan has an even better header at the crosses. So maybe that is the difference. They are both good at link-up [play]. I would say they both have a top mentality, both are two good players.'

Frank may have been reluctant to admit the recipe to his success, but if it is anything, it's his ability to work with strong characters and to bring the best out of them. As well as working to identify players based on data, Brentford scouts are also instructed to conduct background checks on the players. Brentford's recruitment team analyse every new player on their mentality as well and prospective signings are evaluated on a strong criteria. This ensures that Frank has players with the right character and attitude, who can bounce back even from a crushing defeat at Wembley.

Brentford finished the subsequent season with 87 points, six more than in 2019/20. However, even that was not enough for automatic promotion. Once again, their route to the Premier League was through the play-offs – with a tough final against Swansea City at Wembley.

Having become a better team, Frank's side headed in as the favourites, and they didn't disappoint. Bryan Mbeumo burst into the Swansea box just a few minutes into the game and was brought down by the Swansea keeper. Toney took the subsequent penalty and gave Brentford the lead after just ten minutes. Emiliano Marcondes added a second ten minutes later, and that was enough to secure that long-awaited return to the top flight after 74 years.

In their first season in the Premier League, Brentford finished an impressive 13th. The following season, Frank led his team to the top half, finishing ninth. Throughout it all Brentford have continued to invest wisely. Under Benham, Brentford's valuation has skyrocketed. The club has also found a new home, moving from the historic but dilapidated Griffin Park to the much sleeker and modern Community Stadium in 2020.

Despite playing in the Premier League, Brentford hadn't abandoned their data-led approach. The club continues to be innovative in recruitment and explore untapped markets. This includes bringing in players like Kim Ji-soo from South Korean second-tier club Seongnam FC, and Mukhammadali Urinboev from Pakhtakor in the Uzbekistan Super League.

But above all, Brentford have maintained their intrinsic principles. They have remained a tight-knit, family club, motivated for success, but also determined to do it in the right way: to not only develop footballers, but people and characters.

'I think all of us in this club want to perform and want to win football matches,' Frank said. 'But besides that, an important part of that is that we try to develop people and football players. I think that goes hand in hand very importantly and if we develop people and football players, then we also develop the team, hopefully win more matches, but a big part of that is the enjoyment of seeing players develop to an even higher level [and potentially move on from the club], so we follow our boys when they leave their house or their home and go out in the big world and we are very, very proud.'

# 24

# Right to Dream

KAMALDEEN SULEMANA'S legs sprang up from the ground and his lithe body spun mid-air in the Ghanaian Eastern Region sunshine. Just as the young boy was in full flight, Jeremy Seethal's stomach was also spinning. He knew the sensation well. The gut feeling and the rush of excitement. This was the sensation of witnessing a star being born. For a scout, it's a feeling that doesn't come around often.

'Just as he does cartwheels now, he did cartwheels when he scored and the feeling I got was one of cartwheels and excitement,' Seethal recalled in 2021 of the moment he spotted Sulemana.

'It can take months, sometimes years, to find that one player. There was a sheer parallel joy, one for me as the scout, because I've discovered this rare talent and then one for the player.'

Over his long and established career, Seethal has built a track record for discovering 'rare talents'. As well as Sulemana, who has gone on to play in the Premier League and the World Cup, Seethal also discovered the likes of Simon Adingra (Ivory Coast and Brighton & Hove Albion) and Mohammed Kudus (Ghana, Ajax and West Ham United).

Sulemana has been one of the key pillars of Right to Dream, an organisation that focuses on not just scouting and player recruitment but in player development.

Since the 2010s, Right to Dream has become one of the most profitable academies in world football. According to statistics by CIES Football Observatory in 2021, 24 Right to Dream graduates were playing professional football in Europe's top 31 leagues – the same amount as players who have progressed through the ranks at Tottenham Hotspur. The club's academy stars generated more than £100m in transfer fees between 2019 and 2024.

Yet over two decades ago, Right to Dream was merely just a dream by Tom Vernon. He had moved to Ghana as a teenager and discovered an abundance of talent and potential everywhere he looked. Vernon worked as a scout for Manchester United, reporting directly to Sir Alex Ferguson, but he always aspired to do more, to improve more lives and harness the potential of the region. He founded the academy in 1999.

In the beginning Right to Dream started out with humble origins.

The academy's first players lived in bunk beds in the home Vernon shared with his then girlfriend and now wife. It took years for Vernon to build the foundations of the academy before things really started to take off. But his commitment to the project and his determination to make things work paid off in the end.

Vernon's vision ended up being not just a football academy but a boarding school, which offered top-class education and coaching to prospective players on a scholarship basis. Vernon partnered with US boarding schools to help fund Right to Dream.

Some of his first successes included Daniel Owusu, who signed for Fulham in 2006, and steadily Right to Dream's influence grew within the next decade.

From the beginning Vernon had envisioned Right to Dream to be a different sort of academy. Its vision first and foremost has always been to develop human beings, and then footballers.

That is why the academy has focused not only on delivering elite coaching to prospective players, but also offering high-level education. The staff at Right to Dream are just as proud of the players who have gone on to represent their countries at the World Cup as the young people who have gone on to study at Stanford, and other elite US universities.

'As the players move through our system, we have an international academy, which is designed to help those players with a little bit more financial literacy,' Kamaldeen Seethal explained.

'Through the international academy, players are given opportunities to travel. They are then given that opportunity to better look after themselves. And it helps us better prepare players and students [to life in the big world].

'Our students that go to the USA. That's a big thing too, you know. For the record, I think it's important that you also know that as well as players like Kamaldeen [Sulemana], there's also Ousseni Bouda, who in 2011 went from Wagadu to Right to Dream and now he's a Stanford University student.'

As of 2023, Right to Dream has had over 50 graduates studying at either high schools or universities across the US and UK. As Seethal said, this has become another important part of the academy's legacy.

To achieve this success, Right to Dream's approach to player development has been a holistic one. Young players are thoroughly scouted, and their characters are also assessed. When they are brought into the academy, they also have the support system around them, not just on the pitch but off it as well. After all, this is a difficult period for any young person. To be 11 or 12 years old and to live apart from your family, most of the time with strangers, is not an easy transition. There are going to be hurdles and setbacks along the way. But Seethal has insisted at Right to Dream that players always have a shoulder to lean on. Seethal himself remembered crying together with players on the sidelines and showing them his support through difficult moments, 'It's probably one of the most understated things [being away from family] and unfortunately, there's not enough love and care and respect for emotions.

'At Right to Dream one of the biggest things we're trying to teach and to understand is how to emotionally care for the players in the system, which is why we give them a five-year scholarship and we trust them through the periods that they will dip because we know they'll come back up again. We believe that. We believe in our scouting. We believe in our culture, character and school.

'So, when they are having an emotionally tough time, it's also because they don't know how to express their feelings, because culturally your feelings are not something you speak about in Africa.'

In order to deal with the cultural challenges, players have been constantly encouraged to open up. The staff also go above and beyond to support the players. Seethal said Right to Dream even offers support to a player's family where possible, 'It's important that we have a team that understands what an African player stands for and the pressures that are on them. They need to understand what the identity of playing in various countries are, whether that's North or Southern Africa – basically, what's their reason for playing football?'

For Seethal that answer was simple, 'Ultimately, it's underpinned by family and joy. We have a history of exciting role models in Africa with George Weah, Jay-Jay Okocha, Nwankwo Kanu and now Mohamed Salah. It's all players who put you on the edge. If you watch them now, Kamaldeen plays on the edge. Mohammed Kudus plays on the edge and Diomande [Mohamed Diomande, another academy graduate, who moved to Nordsjælland from Right to Dream and signed for Rangers on loan in 2024] plays on the edge. We have players who are very much on the edge. Our job is to make sure that they don't fall off that edge. That's also looking after them culturally. Understanding what their family's needs are, who's important to them. Because if you look after who's important to them, then you look after the most important thing and then you can get them to perform and to be patient.'

In order to help players in the academy system, there is also a dialogue between coaches and the other support staff on a regular basis. This ensures that there is never too much stress placed on an individual. The goal is for every player's needs to be understood and met.

Seethal said, 'We always have the support away from the pitch. It's so important to feed information into the coaches. Because the coaches will have a duty and obligation to get them [the players] up to a performance level and then outside of the pitch there's also another potential, which is the big one, that we look after.

'We have open dialogues with the coaches. There's a lot of constructive criticism that goes on to say, "This is what we saw, and this is what you want." But what we saw is not going to reach the end game, it's not going to be translated into Champions League football unless you allow him to go down and then come back up again.'

That dialogue between coaches, scouts and other support staff has created an environment for young players where they have been able to flourish and bring out their best qualities. For Seethal, he believes this was one of the key pillars behind Right to Dream's success, 'The trust between scouting and coaching is extremely important, I would say, to turn Kamaldeens, Diomandes, Mohammed Kuduses, into the level that they are.'

Right to Dream's success speaks for itself. As of 2023, 67 players, male or female, from the academy have represented their national teams at senior level. Seven players also featured in the 2022 men's World Cup in Qatar.

As the academy's influence has grown in strength, so has Tom Vernon's footballing network. With more money and investment, Vernon was able to purchase FC Nordsjælland in 2016.

Just like at Right to Dream, Vernon and his staff have turned the Danish club into one very much focused on youth development, and integrated that holistic approach into the youth system.

One of the breakout stars of Euro 2020 was Mikkel Damsgaard, who came through the youth system at Nordsjælland and played a key role in helping Denmark reach the semi-finals. He was also joined by fellow Nordsjælland graduates Andreas Skov Olsen and Mathias Jensen in Denmark's squad. All three benefitted from Right to Dream's methods. Meanwhile, Denmark's coach at the tournament, Kasper Hjulmand, spent three years working under Vernon at Nordsjælland.

Other academy success stories include Andreas Schjelderup, who was sold to Benfica and has been widely regarded as one of the most exciting young prospects of his generation.

One of the main benefits of buying Nordsjælland for Vernon has also been the opportunity to create a pathway for Right to Dream's young academy prospects in Ghana to play European football. The likes of Kudus, Sulemana, Simon Adingra and Ernest Nuamah have all made that pathway before signing for clubs in Europe's top-five leagues.

'One of the massive positives of having FCN [Nordsjælland] is that we are able to have a natural progression from the academy's philosophy through FCN, which is aligned,' Seethal said.

It's a partnership and pathway that wasn't an overnight success. But over time, Right to Dream has worked hard to turn it into one of the most successful footballing networks in the sport.

'I think initially when the partnership was young we were learning about each other's cultures and through like a very deliberate integration process we were able to have groups travelling over to Denmark and they were coming over to Ghana,' Seethal explained.

Through a concentrated effort, coaches and academy staff were moved around between Denmark and Ghana to achieve cohesion.

Seethal said, 'Gareth [Henderby] who's the head of academies moved over to Denmark so that helped with the integration process because he's then able to transfer all knowledge from the players who he has worked with from 11, 12 and 13 years old. And then we have Laryea Kingston, who's a coach, Didi Dramani, Michael Essien, Derek Boateng [all of whom work in Denmark]. Derek is the scout, and he and I work hand in hand.'

With so many Ghanaian coaches working in Denmark, Right to Dream have established a safe environment for the academy's graduates to make their first steps in European football. It's an environment which helps them cope with the homesickness and the culture shock of leaving their homeland for the first time.

'It's an important step for integration and to be able to prepare the players,' said Seethal. 'Basically, it's creating a home in Denmark, a little mini-Ghanaian community or African community in Denmark and it's not just creating

Africa there, it's also merging with the Danish culture because if you look at the concept of *hooga*, and the concept of being African essentially, it both means spending time with family. So, we all speak the same language. It just manifests in different ways. So that's our process of bringing that together.'

Having former Ghanaian internationals like Kingston, Dramani, Essien and Boateng, who have all enjoyed professional careers in European football, from Ghana, is also a huge assistance. They are regarded as role models by the young players, and they are able to impart their wisdom on and off the pitch.

Seethal continued, '[Michael] Essien is there because he loves the style of play and he loves what we're doing with changing lives, transforming characters and teaching kids the value of being more than footballers at 18 years old. He knows that that's like everlasting change, as opposed to players that he's played with from Africa at like under-20 level and you know in the Olympics or whatever who've fallen off the map because they didn't have that support network.'

But Right to Dream's programme and education have not been reliant on their presence alone. The players are provided with a comprehensive education. Throughout their time in the academy, Right to Dream aspires to teach kids values and ideals that they can use off the pitch in their everyday lives as well.

'I think our process of development is to work with the understanding that if there is no Michael Essien there, the boys are still self-sufficient in terms of holding their own in a media conference because our character development programme from 11 to 18 has in some ways prepared them to stand on their own two feet.'

In a way, Right to Dream's development style has that of a second parent. The coaches and the educators all share a close bond with each prospective player. But ultimately, Right to Dream have understood that the players needed to be let go and spread their wings. Just like every kid must ultimately leave their parents behind.

Seethal said, 'That's our ethos. We hope whatever we have taught him, you know will be like whispers. It's kind of like parenting. When you're not there, [you have to hope] whatever you've instilled [in them] from a young age they will still do it but also be guided by their [own] values. Sometimes you have to fall too. It's not going to be easy.'

Falling down is part of life. But Right to Dream's holistic approach prepares young footballers better than most.

In the last decade, Tom Vernon's project has grown exponentially. As well as having a club in Denmark, Right to Dream have also opened an academy in Egypt, and bought Egyptian club TUT FC in 2022.

With help of funding from the Mansour Group, Right to Dream also expanded into the US, and established a new MLS franchise club and academy in San Diego FC. In the span of just 25 years, Vernon's vision has gone from an academy being run from his own home to a network that has stretched between three different continents, four countries and generated millions of pounds in revenue.

In a game that has become riddled with players being treated like machines and assets rather than human beings, Right to Dream have set the example to follow. They have shown there is a way to generate income, and develop footballers and people the right way. Tom Vernon's legacy has already made him one of the most iconic figures working behind the scenes in football in the 21st century, but the truth is his legacy has only just begun. With the foundations he has established, Right to Dream will endure for decades and decades, if not centuries.

# Acknowledgements

FIRST OF all, I want to thank the dozens of professionals and experts who took time out of their busy schedules to speak to me over the last four or five years. Without their contribution this book would never have been published.

Above all, I also want to thank my partner, Ula. Without her support over the last few years, this book also wouldn't have been possible.

I also want to thank all my friends and family, including my parents, brothers, and my best friend Kristof and my colleagues in the industry, particularly Tom Underhill and Ninad Barbadikar. A few years ago, we founded a website called First Time Finish. Our original interviews and feature pieces on the website were sourced by some of the biggest websites in the UK, including the Daily Mirror, GOAL. com, the Daily Mail, Metro, Sports Bible, HITC and many others. That website was our break into the industry, and without FTF, this book also wouldn't have been possible.

A special mention to my publishers, Pitch Publishing. They have all been very supportive and helpful during the whole process of this book.

And finally, I want to thank all my followers on my social media, and everyone who bought this book. Your support keeps me going, and I'm very grateful. This book has been a labour of love for many years, and I hope you enjoyed it. If you didn't, I hope I didn't waste your time too much.